Real Estate Rocket Fuel

Mike Carraway

Real Estate Rocket Fuel

Copyright © 2012 by Mike Carraway

ISBN-13: 978-1477443637
ISBN-10: 1477443630

Table of Contents

Introduction

Welcome and thank you again for purchasing Real Estate Rocket Fuel.

It is my goal to make this guide the most helpful and inspirational material you have ever read to bring you into the 21st Century of Real Estate marketing.

Have you ever sat back and looked around at other Real Estate agents that are kicking it in the market and wondered, why are they succeeding at selling, and you are not? What's their secret...what are they saying to their clients that I am not...how do they find all these people that want to buy and sell...are they just in the right place at the right time...were they just born with horseshoes you know where?

They will force you into retirement!

If you have ever had these thoughts then you have just purchased the best material that is going to answer those haunting questions. There has been a shift in the selling market that we used to know and became quite comfortable with. The time has come to step out of that comfort zone and get into the 21st Century way of doing business because they are coming, and they are coming fast. If you don't keep up and move as fast as them then the empire you have built will be up for sale and gone forever.

You know who I am talking about...those wet behind the ears new computer savvy graduates that look like they still need babysitters themselves. Look around...do you see them? Fear them! They will force you into retirement! Why...because they know what you don't. They were born with it and lived with it all their lives. It is second nature to them, and they know the hidden powers it possesses.

**They can cleverly make buyers/sellers
find them and NOT YOU with a few clicks!**

So now is the time to sit down, buckle up, pay attention and get into their game before you get run out of town. Literally, they will take over your town faster than you can write up your next contract. They can cleverly make buyers/sellers find them and not you with just a few clicks. I realized this a long time ago, and I vowed to never let them get ahead of me. I have been in Real Estate for 27 years. I started in 1987 in a small town in Kansas of all places. Back then, and until 2001, we ALL did real estate the same way... Run some ads of a few listings and then try to turn a phone call into a customer. Believe me – I've done it that way for years.

Let me tell you a little bit about who I am and WHY you should read this book.

I started in real estate in 1987, but I didn't really START until 1996. You see – it took me 9 years to "figure it out" and what I mean by that is to figure out what marketing was and setting up a REAL business was. Then, I learned how to automate almost all of the tasks that go with the business. And I DO NOT mean the mundane pre-closing tasks – I mean the "finding prospects" tasks.

Between 1996 and 2001, a short 5-year period, I was one of the top agents in my city. Why? Because I didn't have to prospect – my systems did that for me. In those years, I did almost ½ million in commissions every year in a market that had an average sales price of $145,000 (you do the math).

I started my own real estate company in 1998 (still in business!) and when a new agent would come on board, I would show them my systems and show them how to set everything up.

I started my own real estate school in 2001, which I still maintain today. The real estate school allowed me to pass on some of these techniques and systems to students, who would then join our company. By 2006, we had 2 offices and 75 agents who were Rockin' and Rollin'. Those were some VERY good years.

Currently, I have been chosen by the Alabama Association of REALTORS to be a GRI instructor for technology classes throughout the state of Alabama. I've also trained thousands of REALTORS in Louisiana and Alabama in pre-license, post license and CE Classes.

In a word – I have been teaching and instructing REALTORS in several states for the last 12 years – not to mention all the agents at my own company.

But, there is a side to this story that most people don't know... I also have been marketing products and services on the Internet since 1996. One of my first products went viral in 1997 and to this day can still be found promoted by hundreds of people online. Just do a search on "Multiplying Paid to Real Email Business". If you click on one of the links and read one of the pages, the copy you will see was written by me 18 years ago!

I also run and maintain 3 different "virtual" businesses on the Internet that generate over $60,000/year in profits. These are businesses and websites that run on autopilot, which require capturing leads and then following up, and result in sales.

So, in summary, I know what I am talking about, and YOU should pay VERY close attention to what you are about to learn.

Chapter 1 – Ranking on Google

If buyers are shopping on the Internet, you need to be on the Internet!

If you want more information about _____ anything! Where do you go to find it? Nowadays, if we want to find out anything about anything we go to this information highway called the Internet. Most people - about 90% of the world, do their searches in Google to find things. When people get a notion that they want to buy or sell property, will they be able to find you? Unless you have already read this entire book and put these plans into action then chances are the answer is NO.

Fewer people are out there driving around aimlessly house shopping and writing down phone numbers they picked up from For Sale signs. Instead the trend is for more and more people to house shop without leaving their home. If perspective buyers/sellers are in need of help, you need to be there at the forefront to assist them. You don't want them pulling names out of a hat and hoping it's yours. So, if they are shopping on the Internet then you need to be on the Internet too.

Be on page 1 of Google today!

Having a website is all dandy… having a website that ranks on page one of Google is the cream of your business. Where is your website ranking? Are you on page 1, or are you on page 53,000? You can spend $30,000 for a search engine optimization plan and wait a year to get on page one of Google or you can do what you learn in this book and be on page 1 of Google today. Have you looked at the website www.realestaterocketfuel.com? There's a little video on there that shows you how to get to page 1 on Google for any listing you have. By the end of this book, you will know how to set up your own website where you control all the content and the cost to you to do this is zero. Now that is exciting!

In fact, you can set up 25 websites if you want to. Having 25 listings and having to advertise all them right now really stinks doesn't it? Well, what if you could put them all on the first page of Google for free and not have to pay for it? Would that be something that might interest you? Are you paying a monthly fee for the website you currently have? When you are finished with this book you'll probably go cancel that because you don't need it. You can put MLS feeds, you can put videos, you can put all your listings on your website, and it doesn't cost any money.

If you are on page 53,000 of Google, your Website is worthless. If you are paying a monthly fee, that is an expense you need to lose. If you are on page 1 of Google, and you are paying a monthly fee stay there because you are getting traffic. There's a statistic that says, "it takes 700 visits to your website to get one potential customer, and if you're on page 53,000 you are not going to get 700 visits. You have to be on page one.

A Couple of Things about Google!

There are a few things you need to know about Google with the main one being that there's not really any such thing as a website. Google looks at individual pages and that's important when you have a page that is optimized for a certain keyword string such as Birmingham Real Estate, Trussville Real Estate, Mountain Brook Real Estate, or Mountain Brook Homes for sale. Those are all different keyword strings. If you have a page that is optimized for 1 particular keyword string, your website may never be found unless people type in that one keyword string and then your page will come up.

Another thing about Google is that Google loves old things. Google likes old sites that have been around a long time. I have a site that's on page one of Google for Birmingham Real Estate. Its page has ranked number 4 for years, but it's been there about 15 years. That's one of the reasons why it's on page 1 because Google likes old things. The older your site is, the more Google love you will get. You're going to find it very difficult to compete with these old sites that have been around a long time, especially when your site is relatively new.. Therefore it's better to compete on different terms.

If you do a search on Google for Birmingham Real Estate, you will see that a number that comes up in the top right hand corner and that number is currently 15.9 million. What that means is that there are 15.9 million websites and web pages that are indexed for Birmingham Real Estate. That's your competition! Now that can be scary. How do you compete against that? You can't, unless you want to pay a lot of money or spend 10 years doing it. That being said, let's look at tools we CAN use to help us compete.

Chapter 2 – The Power of Blogging

The first marketing tool we are going to look at is a Blog. You may have seen this word around and you might even have a blog. Have you ever wondered, what's the big deal about Blogs?

A blog is where a business owner can share news about his business!

A blog is a type of website which allows you to update your content in an easy manner. You can compare a blog as a way of updating current news and events.

Here's how Blogs work. Blogs are Websites that are organized by Blog posts. These are individual news stories, like articles in the paper. Bloggers simply fill out a form to post a new story, with a click of a button, the Blog post appears in the top of the Web page, just above yesterday's news. Over time the Blog becomes a collection of these posts all archived for easy reference.

Basically, I am just going to put it a different way, a Blog is a website that you control the content on. You can put up anything you want. You can put up pictures, you can put up videos, and you can arrange the content in any manner you choose. It only takes 3 clicks to set your own blog up. So if you know how to click a mouse you're good to go.

It took 2.5 months to get to page one on Google!

Back to competing, you can compete using different terms. Let's look at an example... If you were to type in Center Point Real Estate, what you would find is the number 3 website is a free Blog. It is a free Blog from one of our Agents. All she did was post on it for about two months, she put information about Centerpoint on it and then put some of her listings up there. Now she's number three on Google for Centerpoint Real Estate. It took 2.5 months to get to page one on Google for Center Point Real Estate... and the reason why... there were only about 600,000 competing sites. That's the first reason. The second reason is Google likes Blogs. In fact, Google loves Blogger because Google owns it. For that reason if you put up a Blog using Blogger.com, it's going to be indexed almost instantly by Google.

Here's another example...type in 304 Liberty Court and when you do, the first 7 or 8 websites are all mine, and they are all Blogs, they are all free and they all have information on that house. All of these first few sites say Liberty Court. That took me about 30 minutes to set up. Can you imagine what my customer thinks? They go to Google and type in their address, and they get all these search results from me. Think that would help you earn a little bit more money?

So now how do you do that? The other thing you might say is who's going to search on the exact address? How do I get people to do that? What do you want me to do, run some Ads? Speaking of Ads, let's take a little side step here. Around 2003-2004 consumers started getting an understanding of this Internet thing. They realized they could go on the Internet and find houses, do virtual tours and look at all the pictures. Why look at a 4- line classified Ad in the newspaper when you can just go on the Internet and see the whole thing? Now jump to 2004-2009 everybody does it! We have all seen newspapers going out of business all over the country and the reason is, their Ad revenue is dropping because you all quit spending money with them. The customers aren't going there anymore instead they're going to the Internet to find exactly what they want.

People will type in the address if you tell them to!

So let's get back to the address thing. People will type in the address if you tell them to. If you title a Blog or a website... the address of one of your listings, there's not going to be any competition for it. You can type in any listing you have and you will probably not find any search results coming up in Google. So, how do we tell people to search on the address?

On all of your flyers, on other sites that you can put your listings on, on your business cards, and even on the SIGN in front of the house – just put "Google The Address For More Info." If you put that in the remarks and somebody reads that they will type in the address in Google. You have just put up six sites so you will be found. They are also going to find the house. Remember you want 700 visitors, so you can capture one lead.

Think where else could you put the term 'Google The Address'. Every single picture you put in MLS has a place for comments and if every single comment said, "Google The Address For

More Info", people are going to do it. If you tell them enough times they will follow your instructions. You can go into Microsoft paint or something similar and bring up your house picture and then just type in the text along the bottom of the picture saying "Google the Address For More Info," save the picture and use this as your picture on MLS. People understand that means search on the address. This will work until your MLS tells you to stop. It's not identifying information and it does not violate the rules of Internet Data Exchange. However, one day they may change the rule but for now you can get free traffic out of it.

Remember these websites are free. Therefore you can have an unlimited number of them. Here is an extra tidbit for you to consider. If you have listings in the same neighborhood you will want to put your website up based on the neighborhood or the subdivision name. If you do that and people search on the subdivision, they're going to find you. If you try to compete against Birmingham houses for sale, Alabama Real Estate or any of those top search terms, it isn't going to work because you will end up on page 53,000. That would be wasting your time and money. There's too much competition out there for those terms already.

You can communicate with your group of people!

Your Blog basically is a place where you can communicate with a group of people - your customer base, your clients and your potential customers. On your website or Blog, what type of information would you want to put on it? You can put messages such as – hey, I'll be on vacation next week so call Beth my partner… here's her phone number. If your customers know where your Blog is, they can see that. Don't bother putting information about yourself, because customers don't care about you. Customers are all about them not you. It would be nice if they did care, but they really don't until they get around to making that kind of decision.

Here's the thing, whoever provides the customer with the most information, is going to win. This is very important to understand. You've got to overwhelm them with data. You want to give them more info than they could ever possibly want and have it all in one place. Listings and contact information are 2 of the most vital pieces of information you need to provide. However; there are other pieces of information you can provide that may just as important.

By making things personal more people are likely to read it. What you need to ask yourself is what is a buyer or seller looking for and can you provide them with all the information in one place. In this industry this is known as 'stickiness' which really boils down to do you have all the stuff?

There are many different Blogging platforms and we are going to look at one of these next.

Chapter 3 – Setting Up Your Blog

A very common blogging platform for realtors is Active Rain. Currently there are about 153,000 realtors on Active Rain. It's free. You can go to www.activerain.com, set up an account, click on join and follow the instructions to start blogging. Mostly, you will be adding typed information, perhaps a picture here and there, plus you can place links to your real Website. You can put your listings up along with any other information that is relevant. The downside to Active Rain is that it doesn't allow you the control you need. You can't move anything around. You can't pick your own theme. It's very generic and just not flexible enough.

Another way that you can set up a blog is by going to www.blogger.com. Google owns Blogger – and that's the one we are going to use today. Remember you can use all of these platforms! The best and the most fantastic platform, but also the steepest learning curve, is WordPress. With WordPress, you can go in and set up your blogs the same way as you do blogger, but it's a little bit more complicated. If you learn WordPress and learn how to use it, you will be awesome. If you don't want to learn all that stuff, use blogger - Blogger is easy.

You can go to www.wordpress.com and set up an absolutely free blog or website. You can also download the software and uploaded it to a host, and then you could do all kinds of things with it. I'm going to give you some examples of what you can do with WordPress but an in depth look at WordPress is way beyond the scope of this book.

Blogger

We are going to use Blogger because it is very user friendly and easy to manipulate. Blogger has a lot of customizable options. It's easy to add video to your blog and it's easy to move elements around on the page. You can change your theme and anything you want. The interface is very intuitive. So how do we set something up on Blogger?

First thing is, get a Google account... Google accounts are free to set up. To get started, visit www.google.com/accounts/NewAccount.

You can use the same sign in for Blogger as you do for Google. When you go into www.blogger.com this is the first page you will see.

In just 3 clicks you will have your own website, and once again it is free.

Click the big orange button that says create a blog. On the next page, you will have to put your e-mail address in, retype it, set your own password, retype your password and then add your display name – this step is very important!

A display name is the name that you are known as in realtor land. For most people, it is their own name. You will want to make sure you use your realtor name because every post that you put on here is going to have your name at the bottom - written by. Next put in the word verification as you see it. The purpose of this is to make sure that you are a real human being and not a robot. Then you will click the big orange continue button at the bottom.

This page is the next-to-last thing that you have to do. The title is very important as well. The title is what will be indexed in the search engine. Here are some examples of titles: Center Point Real Estate, Sudbury subdivision, Birmingham Alabama, 1124 Elm St. If you want to put all your listings up one at a time by address, this is how you do it. You put it where it says title. If you want to try to compete with Birmingham Real Estate, then put that in there. But good luck to you - it will take years. If you want these listings to show up quickly, and I'm talking within 24 hours on page one, then put the address in there.

Take note there are a lot of different ways you can add the address. You don't just put the whole address and say okay well I've used the address, now what can I use? You use variations such as:

304 Liberty Court

304 Liberty CT

304 Liberty Court Chelsea

304 Liberty Court Chelsea Alabama

304 Liberty Court Chelsea, AL 35243

Each variation of address has its own blog. Yes, for every one of them. You set one up for every different variation. Believe me once you get used to this, it takes just a couple of minutes. You can set up five or six of these in 20 or 30 minutes. It's not hard at all.

Your Blog address this could have some importance. This is your URL or Uniform Resource Locator Website address as it is technically known as. Right here is where you type in what you want your Website address to be.

For the address examples above you can use 304 LibertyCourt.blogspot.com, and that will become your website address.

Search engines do put some relevance and some importance on your URL, your website address. Therefore, if my blog title is 304 Liberty Court, it would be a really good idea to put 304

Liberty Court here to. The title is going to be the title that shows up when you visit the page, it's going to be everywhere. This is going to be in your address bar in the top portion of your browser. You can use hyphens in there if you want to because the search engines don't see them. You pick a title that best suits your needs for whatever you're trying to optimize your page for. In other words, the search term you want people to type in so this page will come up. This could be the address of your listing, or the name of the subdivision.

You can change a title, but you can't change the address. If you mess up, just delete it and go do another one. You don't have to worry about it.

You can add different information daily. In fact, that's what you want to do, because the more content you add regularly the more Google sees you have made a change. Changes and additions are good. Every time you add something to your Blog, it does something called pinging Google. Basically what this means is that Google is notified of new content. This is an invitation to Google who will then come and look at what you have just added. Google sends out their little search engine spiders to go look at your site again. So if you add content daily to your blog you will get tons of visits from the Google Spiders – this is a good thing! Chances are your rankings are going to be higher by doing this. Remember these are free so just play with it, goof around a bit it won't matter. Put testing 123 and delete what you practice.

Once you are comfortable with the process your next step is to choose a color scheme to determine the look and feel of your site. You can select from the choices shown below:

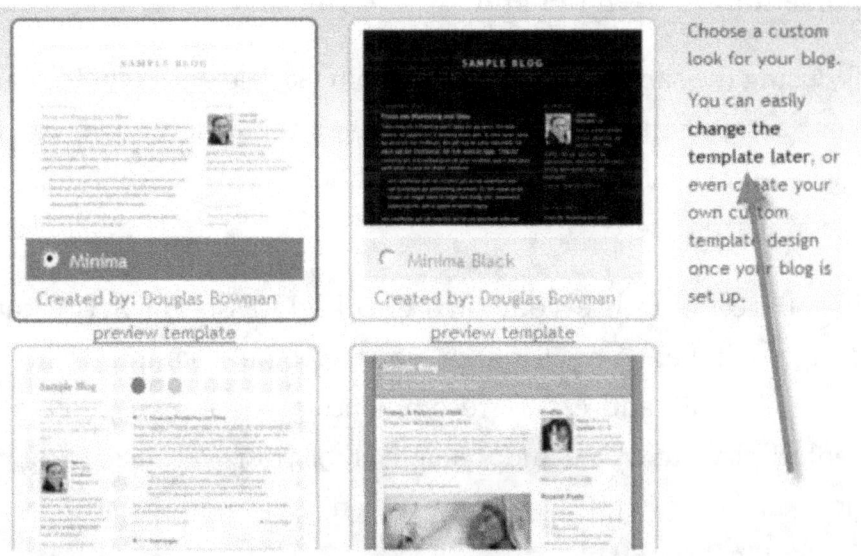

Then there's a big finish button at the bottom. So three clicks, and that's the next screen you'll see.

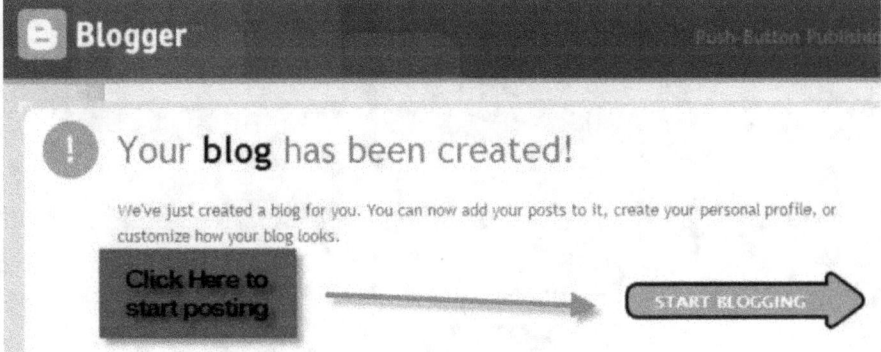

Let's sum that up. You click create, you fill in your e-mail address and your password, you add your title and then select a theme, and you're done. Now there is the easiest creation of a website you'll ever see in your life.

Something to keep in mind...

By using the same e-mail address from Google once you log into your account all of your Blogs are displayed. This allows you to easily edit as many as necessary without having to log into each account separately.

If you decide to use your own email address, which you can, you won't be going through your Google account. Using a Google email address is recommended as it gives you one central place to create and manage all of your websites. Imagine how much easier this will be when you need to add fresh content to 20 or 30 blogs!

The next big orange arrow says start Blogging. Click and then you will see this page.

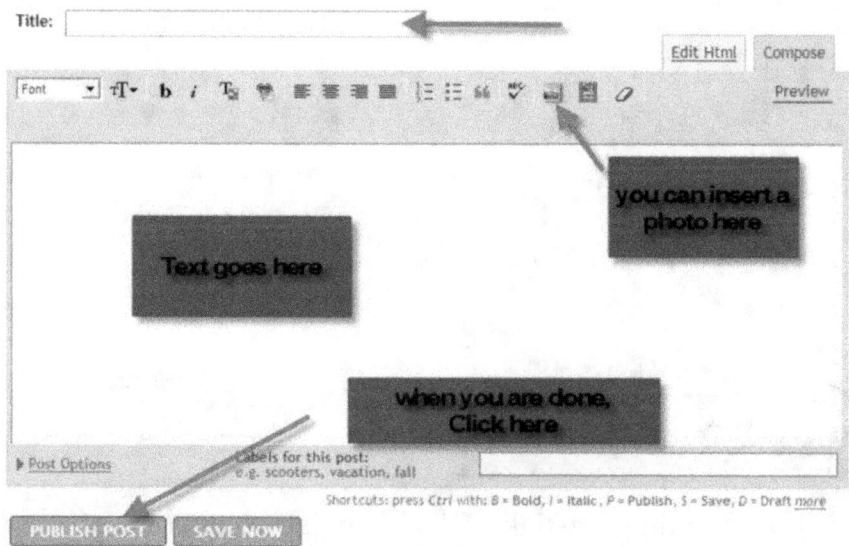

You put in a title and then start typing. When you are done you hit publish post - it will display on your Website. Just like magic.

In the following example I put 'New Home Community Comes to Eastlake' as the title.

They are flooding Eastlake. There's going to be a lot of water-front property there. The Eastlake area of Birmingham is about to undergo big changes and new home community called the Neighborhood is about to start construction.

Adding Your Own Pictures

When you take photographs of a house you are most likely using a digital camera. These photos are downloaded and stored onto your computer. All that is left is to upload them directly to your Blog. As you upload the pictures you can label them the kitchen, the bathroom etc. If your title is 304 Liberty Court the pictures you upload will be specific to that home. This is the type of information people want to see, believe me. The more photographs the better.

To add a picture in there you click on the little picture button and a little window will come up and says - upload picture, and it will have a browse feature. Click on browse and it will let you pick the picture file to upload. Once uploaded you hit save and the photo is inserted into your post.

If your picture and text don't line up properly, go back in and edit it by clicking on this little pencil.

You click on that, and it will take you right back to where you can edit the page.

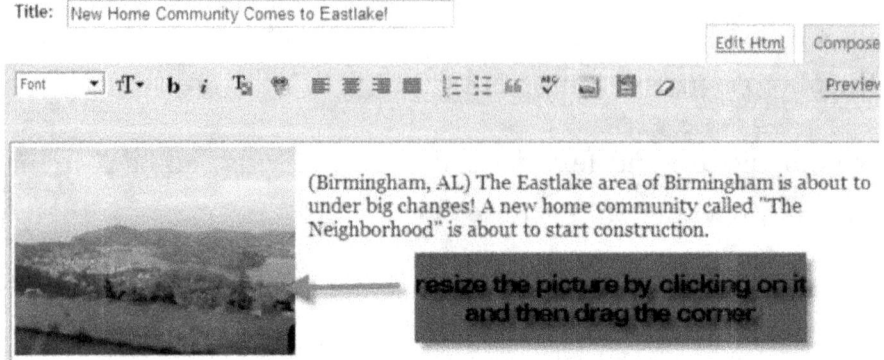

When you click on the image a dotted border appears allowing you to make changes. You simply click on the actual photograph and drag the corner to resize it. Dragging it in this way keeps the image in proportion. Once you are happy with your changes you hit publish again and your page looks good.

People want data and they want to see videos and photos of the house. The more information you place on your Blog the longer your visitor is likely to stay on your page. If they like what they see your chances for capturing a lead improve.

On the post page where we put our title in about East Lake and where we put our picture in, there are little tabs at the top of that.

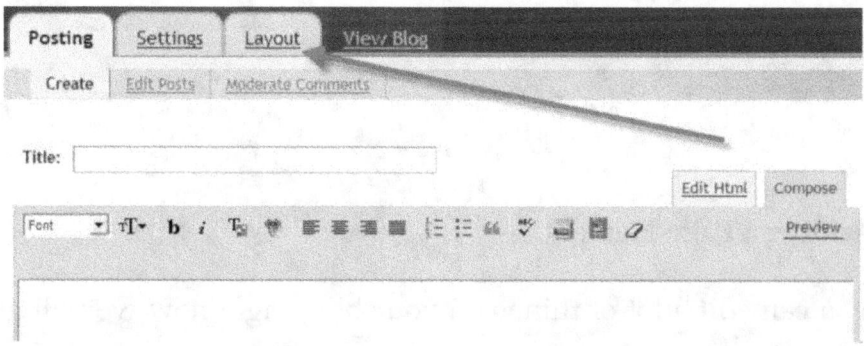

The layout tab is where we can design and make the Blog look like we want it to look. Click on layout, it's says - add and arrange page elements. Here is where you can add a page element, edit your title, edit your profile and put in your own information such as professional accomplishments.

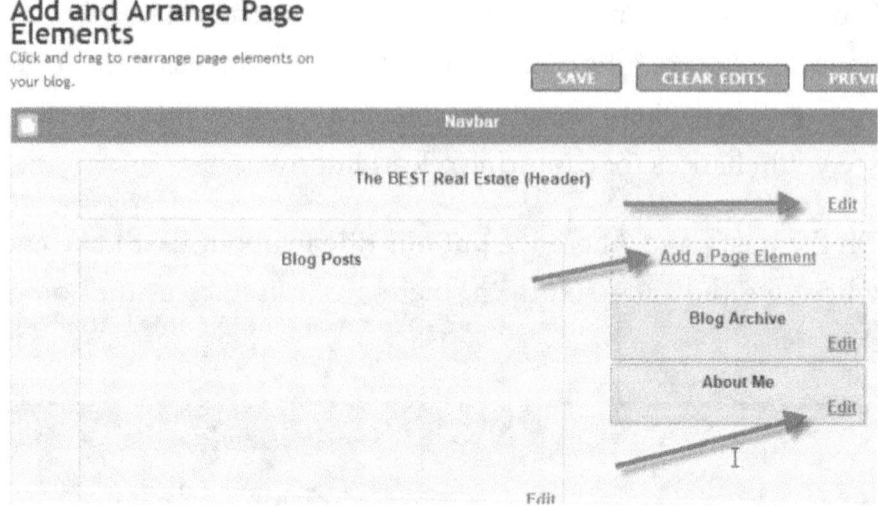

Adding a Page Element

You can edit a lot of things on your blog, right now we will go through adding a page element. Page Elements can also be referred to as Gadgets. The most versatile function on here is also the one that sounds scary, HTML, JavaScript. You don't have to learn programming. This is very important to learn because if you can figure out how to do this, you can put virtual tour's, you can put videos, you can put lead capture forms, you can add all kinds of tools and gadgets on your blog if you just learn how to do this, one thing. All you have to know is how to copy and paste.

All you need to do is find some code and copy it and paste it into this box

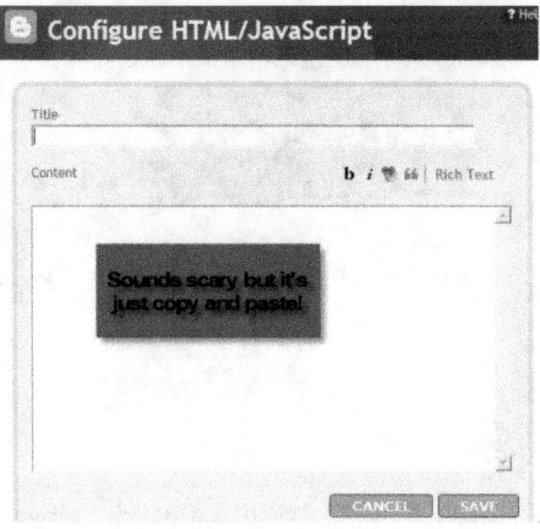

and then hit save.

Let me give you an example using YouTube. I typed in funny Real Estate commercial and all the YouTube videos have something called embed where you see the arrow pointing below.

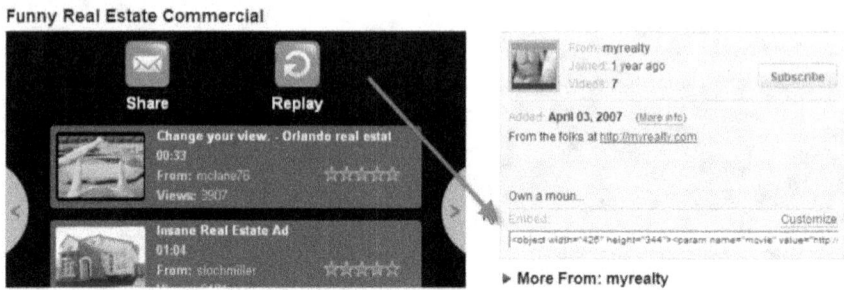

Next you want to highlight the embed code and then use Control + C to copy the code. The code is highlighted and you place your cursor back inside this box.

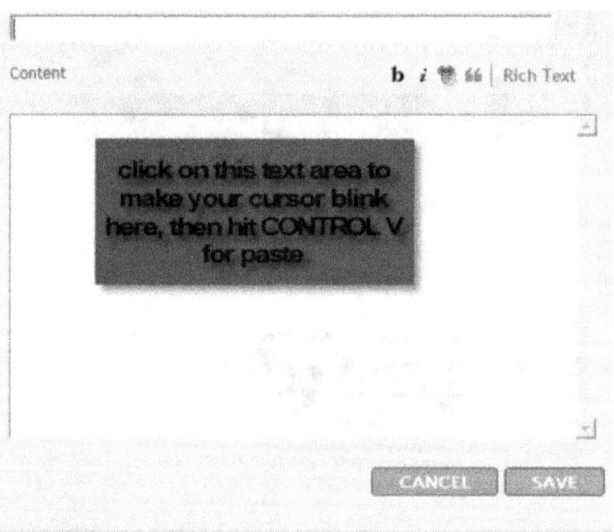

You will paste the text by using Control + V. The You Tube code is placed directly into the box. This is what it will look like:

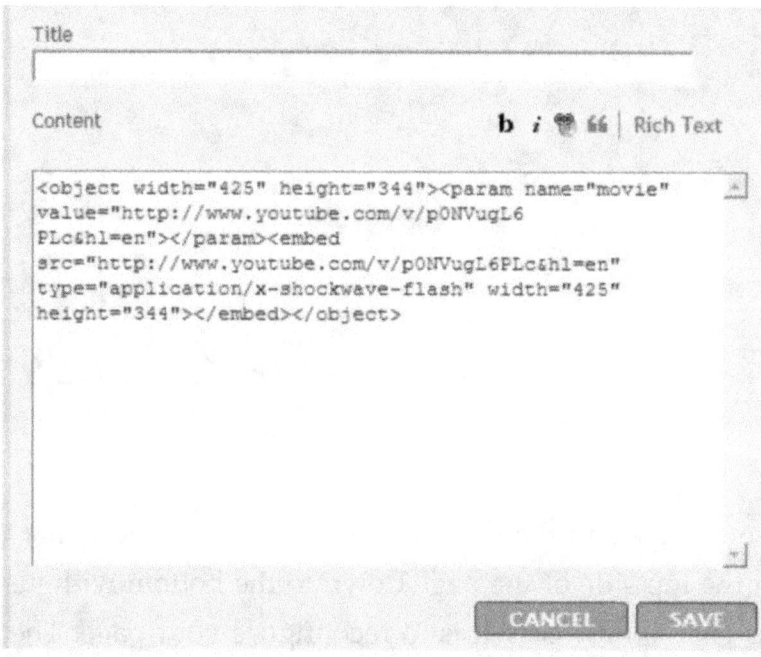

Your next step is to hit save and you have now embedded a video onto your blog. There really is nothing more to it than that!

Elements can be moved around on your page as well. You can click on it and drag it down to a new position.

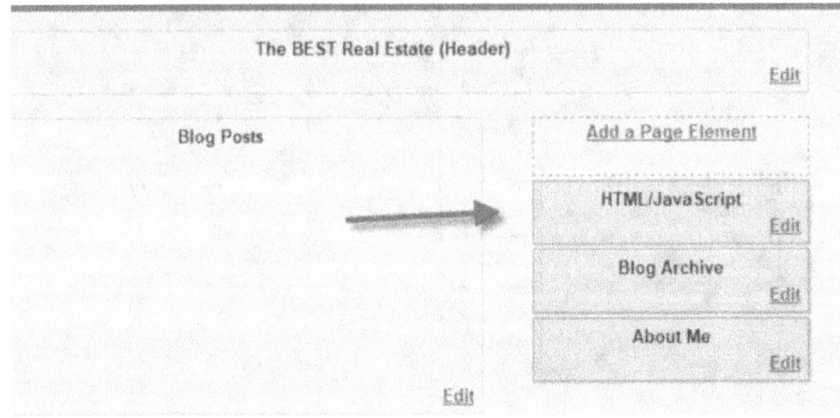

As you can see in the diagram we have now moved the video from the top side of the page down to the bottom with just one click. That is how easy it is to reconfigure your page. The code that you just placed inside the HTML/Java Script could have been code for a virtual tour! It would be great to offer virtual tours on your website wouldn't it?

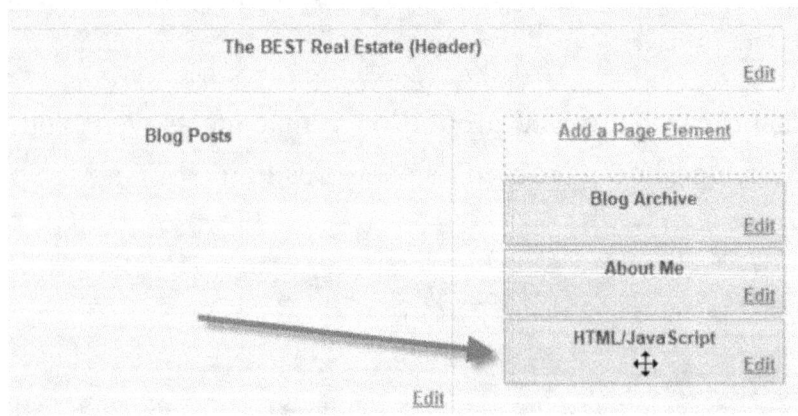

Something to keep in mind – When you are copying someone else's material you need to give credit to the author and provide a link back to the author's site. It's always best to send them an e-mail and get permission. Most of the time they are going to allow you to use their content, especially if you offer to link back to their site. This is known as back linking and helps to increase the popularity of their site, which is one of the reasons most people will agree to you using their material.

The more links you have coming into your site from other sites the more the search engines will pay attention to you. A site with more content on than anybody else is known as an authority site. This is another major factor in getting more traffic to your site and increasing your popularity. Remember what I said earlier, overwhelm them with data - add as much information on there as you can think of.

Here's a look at our finished blog:

New Home Community Comes to Eastlake!

(Birmingham, AL) The
Eastlake area of
Birmingham is about to
under big changes! A new
home community
called "The
Neighborhood" is about to
start construction.

POSTED BY MIKE CARRAWAY AT 10:49 AM   0 COMMENTS

Subscribe to: Posts (Atom)

▼ 2008 (1)

  ▼ June (1)
      New Home Community
      Comes to Eastlake!

ABOUT ME

MIKE CARRAWAY

VIEW MY COMPLETE PROFILE

Chapter 4 – Valuable Information Flow

What Does A Customer Want?

The number one thing a customer wants is information on houses. You can easily provide lots of information by setting up a main site, which is something I highly recommend you do. This site will not be optimized for just one address. Instead you may want to optimize it for Birmingham homes for sale now. I actually used the word 'now' as a way to rank higher in the search engines.

Remember the longer your keyword phrase is the more likely you are going to rank number one for that phrase, as long as you have the title of your site with the same name. Keywords are so important, I can't stress that enough!

Your customer's are looking for information on various homes for sale in a particular area. Therefore it makes sense to link directly to the MLS listings, so they can search them. This is known as a gateway feature.

To do this go to the far right hand side on MLS, click on set up, and you can then purchase the gateway product. This will be a link that you paste into your blog in the HTML JavaScript box. Above this you want to put 'search'. You do not want to put the MLS search system. Instead your goal is for your customer to search all the active listings in the Birmingham area.

Note: It is a violation of MLS rules to use the term MLS on any of your websites.

Other neat features to have on your blog are loan calculators such as a mortgage calculator and a loan payment calculator. To find suitable ones just do a search on Google for 'loan calculators for my website'. All you need do is copy and paste the code into the HTML JavaScript box and save it. This is so easy to do and makes your site look more professional. Plus it gives customers a reason to stay longer on your page!

Other things to include are:

Everything about your community

Local weather

Tax rates

Biggest employers in the area

Employment rates

Parks

Recreation

Movie theaters

Favorite restaurants

Favorite dance clubs

Shopping Malls

Schools

Tourism

Medical Facilities

Museums

Golf courses

Events

Fill it up with community information. If I was from Timbuktu, and I was thinking about moving to Birmingham, and I happened to find your website, you need to provide me with everything I want to know about Birmingham. If I don't have to leave your website, and I can get it all there, why would I go anywhere else? Then, when I finally get around to thinking about needing a realtor, you're already there. People like this type of information because it's a recommendation from you.

Info on you is the last thing they want, but you're going to give it to them anyway. You're going to have a little profile section with your picture on there somewhere. The bulk of the information needs to be interesting things they need to know about. The best way to find out what is interesting to people is to ask people. Some of us have been in the business a long time, and we think people want certain things, and they could not care less. Find out what they really want by asking your customers and clients. What do you look for on the Internet - what are the things you would like to see on my website - what would make it easier for you to hunt for houses? Ask them, because that will tell you what content to put on your site.

Capturing Their Information

This is where the money is. If you are buying leads, you are letting somebody else do this work for you, and you're paying for an e-mail, an address or a name and a phone number. All they are doing is setting up lead capture pages for free, and they're selling the information to you. How about we cut them out? If you want to do a significant amount of business then here's the thing… if you don't learn this and apply it, eventually you'll have to buy every lead that you get.

Have you seen the Home Gain sites? This is one of the many companies out there that are lead capture companies. Their profit model is to sell us leads. I prefer to generate my own for free. Are we thinking the same thing here? What you have to have is a way to capture this information. People aren't just going to say… oh, here's a form, I think I will put my name and e-mail in there. They just are not going to do that.

You need to compel them to do that. You have to have something that they want, and it has to be something of value that they need now. What it will be is valuable information that is going to solve their problem. You can find a lot of this type of information on the Internet. For example special reports that show "how to avoid the six biggest mistakes that could cost you

$10,000 when you buy a house." If I am a home buyer, I would want to know what those six big mistakes are. If I can get it free just by giving up my name and e-mail address, and it gets e-mailed to me - I am going to gladly give out my contact information.

If you went to www.RealEstateRocketFuel.com and ordered the first four chapters of the book... you would have had to put in your name and e-mail address to get it. That is a lead capture form. It's called an ethical bribe. It's basically a trade - I'll give you what you're looking for if you give me your name and e-mail address so that I can follow up with you. Whatever you are offering – has to be good. It can't be just junk. It also has to be filled with content. If you offer them something, then don't give them something that is thin and doesn't have meat to the content. There are way too many sites out there missing the whole benefit of gathering contact information. By not gathering contact information they are leaving money and business on the table for someone else to pick up.

The number one thing that people want is unrestricted access to MLS. It doesn't make sense to give people that for nothing. They want it bad enough to give you their contact information so take advantage of this. You have to have a page that they come to that says first... get all the information you want right now - get free unrestricted access to the entire list of listed homes for sale in Birmingham. Fill in your name and your e-mail and click submit... when they do, it will take them to the next page, which will be your search page. That way you're getting something out of it.

Capture Form

A form is just something they can fill out. Here is another free site I am going to send you to - www.emailmeform.com. This will allow you to set up a form to gather their contact information.

Something to keep in mind - do you think it's a good idea to ask them for their phone number? Here's a rule on that - the less you ask for - the more accurate it is. If you start asking for too much information none of the information is going to be real. It's apt to say 123 Anywhere St. if you try to get their address. You want a name and email and that's it. You don't even need the last name.

Your free form will look like this:

Web Form Creation Wizard - Step 1

Designing your web form is simple and easy.
First, you need to create a "thank you" page on your website, to show your visitors after the form has been submitted.
Then, you must enter the Form Name, the email address where you want to receive form submissions, the "thank you" page address (such as http://www.mysite.com/thankyou.html) and the number of fields in the form.

your blog address

Web form Name:	Contact Form for blog	*(To tell them apart in your form list.)
Recipients Emails:	Mike Carraway <its4real4u@aol.com>	*(Max 10 separated by comma. More info)
Spam Email address:		*(Spam submissions will be delivered here.)
Thank you page:	birminghams-best-real-estate.blogspot.com	*(Display to visitor after form submission.)
Number of fields:	3 *(The total number of fields contained by the form)	

Next

The Web form name is where you are going to put "Get Your Free Report Here," or something related to what you are giving them for free. Then your e-mail goes in next and then the thank you page is your blog address. What you want them to do is fill out that form, click submit, and stay on your page. This is whatever your blog address is - something.blogspot.com. Number of fields should be two. This is going to generate a form code that I can copy and paste into that HTML JavaScript box.

There are 9 steps on this e-mail me form to set it up. You just click next, next, next, next until you get to this one.

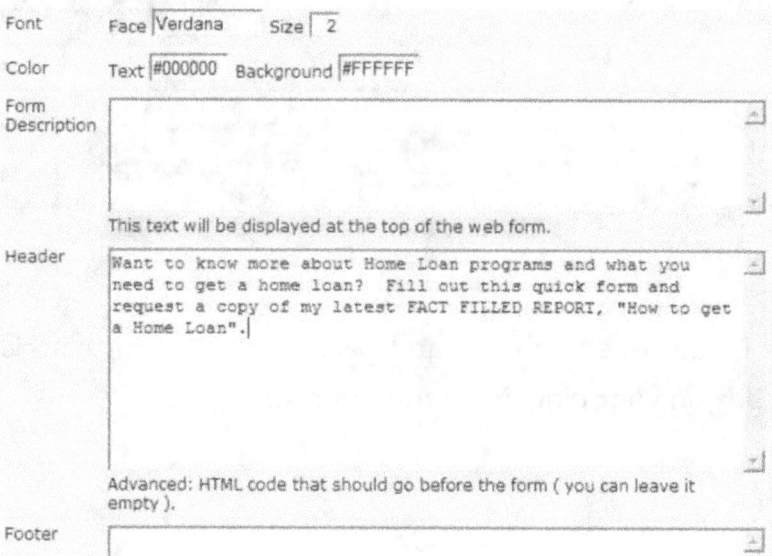

This is the header which is what goes above the form and acts as a title. This is the place where you add your sales pitch.

'Want to know more about home loan programs, and what you need to get a home loan? Fill out this quick form and request at copy of my latest fact filled report, How To Get a Home Loan.'

Many people don't fully understand home loans and there is plenty of information out there which can be confusing. Providing your visitors with information on home loans is a great idea, plus you will see that people will gladly fill out your form to get access to it.

After you click finish you will be given the code for the form.

Web Form Creation Wizard

copy this - highlight then Control C

Your form has been saved!

The web form is active, and ready for use by your visitors. Every submission will result in an email delivered to your email address with the content of submission!

You can see the form on our site at: http://www.emailmeform.com/fid.php?formid=102086

You might want to Get the HTML Code to paste in your site or you might link directly to the form on our site using the code below:

```
<a href="http://www.emailmeform.com/fid.php?formid=102086"
target="_new">Contact Form for blog</a>
```

You may go back to the view the forms list

This is the code you copy and paste back over in that HTML Java box on your blog. Next add your title.

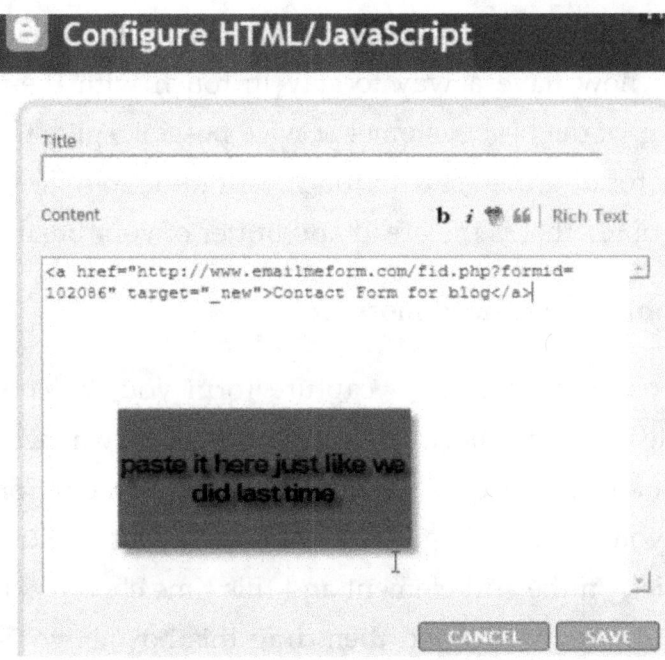

Don't forget to save it. You can now preview what your form looks like.

After someone fills out the information the e-mail will come to your inbox, and it will say form request or information request or form submission. When you see that title, you will know you just got a lead. At this point you are going to send them the report that they just requested.

You already have this report saved on your computer as a PDF file. Attach it to an e-mail and e-mail it to them with something such as 'Attached is your free report on how to get a home loan' as your title.

Now, you can follow up with these people. The whole thing is that you now have a way to stay in touch with them. If you want to give the best customer service possible, give them what they ask for and then stay in touch. Continue to follow up with these people - that is the bread and butter of your business.

One Problem – we need more...

After looking at your new capture form you will notice that your sales pitch is short. A longer sales pitch will work much better in enticing people to sign up for your free report. To do this all you need do is go back into the layout section of your blog. Click on the add element and this time choose a Text Box. Add a little more text and then drag this box above your capture form and click on save.

Here's an example of a longer sales pitch:

These days, getting a home loan is more complex than ever before, there are some big pitfalls that could end up costing you tons of money. Don't let this happen to YOU. Get my free report on how to get a home loan and get it now. This is a little more detailed about the benefits they're going to receive.

Something to keep in mind - There's a book written back in the 30's called Scientific Marketing, read it. If you're into marketing and yes we are in marketing, and you haven't read that book, get it and read it, it's free. Look up scientific marketing on Google, you will find a free copy – download it and read it. Basically, it encompasses four things that an ad has to have in order to evoke a response. It has to get the reader's attention. It has to peak their interest. It has to build their desire for whatever it is that you have to offer them. The four-step process is attention, interest, desire, and action. Everything that you write to try to get a lead needs to focus on those four things concepts.

Automatically Post New Listings

How would you like to have automatic content posting on your blog, without you doing a thing? After the initial setup you can basically forget about it and have new listings automatically publish on your blog.

Let's say your goal was to capture the market in Pelham for $300,000 to $400,000 houses. The first thing you would do is to set up a blog that says $300,000 to $400,000 houses in Pelham. You would set up a blog saying Homes in that price range, especially the ones that are just coming on the market. There is an automatic feature in MLS that is a prospect search, and it mails out listings to your prospects. You must use this or you will be missing the boat.

This feature is easy and the system will send you a copy of the email as well. This way you know exactly what your customers are getting. Now, don't tell your customers this service is free. Instead tell them you spend a lot of time and money to provide this service to them. You may get the odd person who tells you they got their emails at 2 am, your reply is that you were up searching at that time of the night.

Now the way to set all this up is a secret. Did you know that your Blog contains what I like to call a Special email address, and it will automatically post to your blog?

The way to do this is by going into MLS and setting up a new prospect, you want to name this prospect my blog.

Then go back into your blogger account and click on the settings tab. You will notice several subheadings, you want the one that says email.

Once you click on the email tab you will see your blogger username.

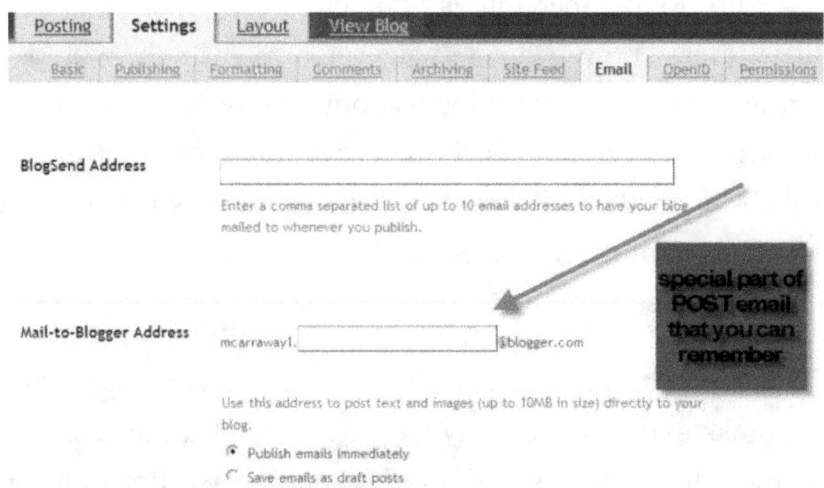

You fill in your special part of the email address before the, @blogger.com. Just make sure it is something easy to remember. You now have a special blog post email address. For example mine could be mcarawa2@blogger.com. So the special e-mail address that I can send posts to blogger for me would be mcaraway1.mcaraway2.@bogger.com

When I send an email to that address it will automatically post it to my website. The subject of the email shows up as the title of the post and the body of the email is the content. You can set this up for every blog you have if you would like to publish content automatically.

Let's go back to the example of targeting $300-$400,000 houses in Pelham. Our goal is to return homes that are listed in this price range. When we do our search, we are going to search for

$300-$400,000 houses in Pelham. You are then going to save your search results and send them to the prospect which you just set up. Remember this is your blog, and that prospects e-mail address is whatever you set up - mine would be mcarraway1.mcaraway2@blogger.com. Now MLS is going to send out e-mails which match these criteria. These go directly to my website or blog. Every day, the new houses that show up will be posted at the top of the page.

You set it once and you can forget it for a little while but what will happen after 15 or 20 posts those searches will expire. Some of the links expire so you have to go in and clean up your blog later by deleting some of the oldest one. These links are only good for 30 days.

You can do a test run for yourself. Go to your regular email account and create a new message. Your blog address goes in the To: section. Then type in a subject line and add some text for the body. Click send and then check your blog. Your email now shows up as the top post on your blog. This works as though MLS is sending the e-mail. The email will contain all the links to all the new listings, and it's going to show the price and the address, plus all of this is done automatically. This was all achieved just by sending an e-mail in MLS and making your prospect your blogs e-mail address - your special posting address.

THE BEST REAL ESTATE

TUESDAY, JUNE 24, 2008

This is a test post for the Blogging CE Class

Amazing things can be done with a blog!

Mike Carraway

Broker/Owner

www.Join-Weichert-Realtors.com

www.BirminghamRealEstateSchool.com

POSTED BY MIKE CARRAWAY AT 11:31 AM 0 COMMENTS

HOW DO I GET A HOME LOAN?

These days, getting a home loan is more complex than ever before. AND, there are some big pitfalls that could end up costing you tons of money. Don't let this happen to YOU!

Let's recap. Go into your blog – settings - click on e-mail. Add your blog name as your prospect. Go back into your Blogger account and add this address as a prospect. Go back into MLS and do your search for your selected criteria. Add your blog as your prospect and send them your search results.

These listings will then match your prospects requirements. These posts will show up automatically for approximately 30 days. Don't forget to check for expired links and make appropriate changes.

You now have automatic content for your site, what could be easier?

Ways You Can Use This

Mobile devices including cell phones allow you to send text messages and emails from anywhere. This is a great tool to have and allows you to post literally from any place any where! You can very well be sitting on the beach, in a waiting room or at the airport. You can quickly and easily send an email and post to your blog. Note: Your device must have the capability to send emails.

This method is great to use if something unexpected comes up. You may be out of town travelling or have an unexpected emergency. Your business will not suffer. You add new content to your blog and no one has to know that you weren't in your office.

Using your main website to update customers is a smart move. This page is where you have all of your content, not just your lead capture page. It should be a power house full of information! This is the site where you can post messages such as...I'm out of town unexpectedly, please call my partner Beth, she can take care of you while I'm away. You can have Beth's contact information on there. You can update your customers and clients as to what you're doing right now at anytime from your cell phone.

You can also update list prices via your cell phone too. You may be at a seller's house, and you finally get that price reduction, you know the one that was overpriced by $50,000, and it had been sitting for four months. You finally get the price reduction and as soon as the seller signs it, you get on your phone, and you type in - house at 123 Elm St. - just reduced $50,000, new list price is, and you click send.

You then tell your seller that you just updated your blog with this information. You can actually show him the page on your cell phone and he will be amazed. He will love that fact that you worked fast and this makes you look good in his eyes. He is sure to recommend you to his friends!

Something to keep in mind – Information regarding mentioning a URL, which is website address, was added to the code of ethics. What this means is that you cannot have a website address that says one thing and when people click on it and visit it, it's about something else. For example, you cannot reserve the URL freehouses.com unless you have free houses. You can't go and reserve ronjacobs.com and have him come to Mike Caraways' website. That's a violation of the code of ethics. I just want to make it clear that whatever website address you have, it needs to indicate pretty clearly what the content is.

Chapter 5 – Your Blog as a Website

Purchasing Domain Names

You may not like the way these domains look – 304 LibertyCourt.blogspot.com or sanduskeyvalleyhomesforsale. blogspot.com. They are quite long as well as being hard to remember and not good to put on a business card. Thankfully there is something you can do about it. You can reserve or buy a domain name for about $7 a year. You can get them for two years for $15 or you can purchase several names at one time and save even more money. If you buy a name and end up not using it you could possibly resell it later for a profit.

When you get a domain name you want it to be short and easy to remember. The shortest domain name I have seen was www.pe.com - now that is easy to remember. The shorter the domain name is the better. If you need to make it a bit longer like www.yourbusinessInternetorname.com you can. That's a bit long, but as long as it makes sense to people in their head it's okay. Domain names are the 800 numbers of the 21st century. I advise you to get a few of them. This is how people find information these days - so a 1- 800 number is good to have, but lots of domain names are even better, especially, if they say things like findahouse.com.

What I would suggest you do is type in Google search- cheapest domain registration, least expensive, cheap domain, and you're going to have some pretty inexpensive domains. Shop around because you can reserve a domain name for $15 for two years. If somebody's charging you more than that you're probably paying too much.

Something to keep in mind - If you have a domain name, and its getting traffic - don't let it expire. Renew it for two more years because that traffic is going to go with the domain name. If somebody else buys it, they've got all your traffic and your Google ranking.

Forwarding Your Domain

After purchasing your domain name you will have an account with that company. Inside this account you can manage all of your domains. One neat feature with a domain name is that you can forward another site to it. The easiest way to understand this is to compare it to call forwarding. You forward your calls from one number to another.

Domain forwarding is the same. You set an end target or landing spot for your visitor to arrive at. When a person types in your new domain name they will end up on your blog or website over at blogspot.com.

To do this inside your domain account there will be an area that says something similar to Manage Your Account. Next, look for a section that says domain forwarding or forward my domain. When you click on this it asks you for a website address, type in your blogger address here and save your changes. Your domain name is now forwarded to your blog. This sometimes takes a few minutes or hours to take effect.

If you have trouble with this process there should be a tech support feature in your account. You may be able to call, ask for help online or you may need to send in a support ticket. They will be happy to help you forward your domain for you.

Your domain name now looks more professional and it will be easy for customers to remember.

One thing that will happen is when your customer types in your new domain name the address bar in your browser will display YourName.blogspot.com.

This doesn't really matter because your main concern is that the customer ends up on your website. It is possible to hide this with something called masking. Many times there is a fee for masking, so it is up to you if you would like to add this feature. It is normally done when you set up your forwarding, which is free.

In Summary

Forwarding your domain name takes your customer to whatever blog or website you specify. You can forward a domain to any site you wish. This isn't absolutely necessary and you are fine with using blogger and adding content to it. My methods will still work for you. A domain name does look more professional though and is a relatively cheap way to create a business image.

Sample Blogs

At this point you should now have at least one main blog and several individual blogs with your property listings. You may also be wondering how much time you should spend blogging. For the individual listing blogs you only need to put up a post or two a month. The main content is added when you first set up these blogs. You add the photos and descriptions along with an email form for them to ask questions or to receive more information. Emailing prospective customers brochures straight from MLS is a good idea too.

Your main blog is where you want to have all your content and this site should be kept up to date. Remember the Google spiders will visit more often if you regularly update your blog with fresh content. You don't have to make major changes, just edit a listing add a new photo or post about a new local event.

Using your individual property listings will be the easiest way for to get traffic. But the important thing is that you need traffic immediately and not two months down the road. The following blogs are ones I currently use to create traffic and to stay in contact with customers.

My Active Rain

Active Rain has a set format - you cannot move items around. You can add links, you can put articles in there, and you can put pictures of the property in the body. Most people that are members of Active rain are either lenders or realtors. However, if you title your articles correctly, and people search on that, it will be indexed in Google, so they might be able to find you. It's just not as effective as some of the other means. I have several articles or posts that provide good information for my visitors. I've got an article on a code of ethics violation that I actually found on another website and put it over here so realtors could see it.

Yes, this is more of a colleague network type website. However, with that being said if you title your articles correctly you may get traffic from this site. It is your title that will help you get indexed into the search engines for any particular search term.

You can see how much time I spend posting on these here: http://activerain.com/action/blogs/comments/33348

There is one post from June 15, 2 on June 17, June 26th, the 29th, and the 30th. These are kind of close together, but I haven't posted anything on this for probably six months. But it's still there… it's still got my phone numbers along with my address. People can find a map to my office and they can e-mail me all from within that site.

My Blogger

Here is my main blogger.com blog http://access1000.blogspot. com it was set up in 2005. You can see how many posts I actually did in 2005… It shows 29. I did 20 posts in 2006, 4 in 2007 and 5 in 2008. That shows you how much time I spend blogging. Yet, you can find this blog just by going into Google and typing in keywords like Birmingham houses for sale. It will come up on page 1 or sometimes page 2 depending on which search term you use. This has been around 4 years… so the longer you're there the better.

I've embedded a video about our real estate school on there. There is a link list which is another gadget on Blogger that you can put on your blog. When you find a link you like, you just copy and paste it into the link list.

These blogs are all our agents' blogs which they set up themselves. All of their pages have links to the other pages too. We've got a little web of blogs about different parts of town, and they're all interlinked. You can do that with your own sites, and you can do it with other agents in your office. The more links that you have going to each other, the more popular your site is. You get a blogging group in your own office and everybody puts up their own blog and then you link them all together. Google will look at these and see all these sites pointing to your site. This makes your site look like an authority site, which means Google will rank you higher and send you more traffic.

On these blogs, you can also put up audio files. You can save an MP3 file and allow people to play it right from your blog. This is done with another one of those gadgets from Blogger.

The first thing I want people to see is my lead capture form. In Internet marketing terms this is called a landing page or a squeeze page. The idea is to squeeze their information out of them. You want to position this form at the top of your page so people see it as soon as they land on your page. This is the best way to capture a lead.

Your goal for your visitor is to provide them with enough information so that they stick around on your site. You can do this by providing them with lots of good content for free. As you can see I only have one thing on my whole site that requires them to fill out a form. Everything else they have access to is free. If they want to learn how to beat other buyers to the best listings, they have to fill that form out.

What we are trying to do is establish a conversation with these customers. Commenting is enabled on all these blogs. It is possible to disable comments but this isn't recommended. This means that anybody that comes to your website can comment on something you wrote. That starts a conversation and you can comment back to them, many people will ask questions this way. You don't have their e-mail or any personal information. They feel like safe to make a comment, and you can comment back, which starts a bonding conversation. They may possibly turn into a lead.

With comments you have the ability to delete inappropriate comments. You can find this option in your settings tab under comments. Comments are useful for providing a dated history of content. As you can see there is a whole history of information dating back to 2005 that is available for viewing to anyone that comes to my blog. If you start reading in 2005 you can see the evolution, and what I've been doing.

My WordPress Blog

www.RealEstateRocketFuel.com

This is a WordPress blog which actually looks like a regular website, but it's nothing more than a blog. It is not your run-of-the-mill static website. It has graphics along with a lead capture form and all kinds of neat stuff. The owner of this site can post fresh content whenever they wish.

This WordPress site took me 45 minutes to put up, which isn't very long. I have a lead capture form along with a buy now button for DVDs, plus a video, lots of articles as well as posts and other pages that people can check out. WordPress is an awesome platform to use but is also a whole other book in itself. For all intents and purposes, you're just as well off as using blogger for your platform as WordPress. If you want to get really pretty and add a lot of bells and whistles then you might want to take a look at WordPress. You go to WordPress.com and sign up for an account, and you'll get a blog on WordPress. It's not quite as customizable, but it looks better than blogger, and it's also free.

http://www.how-to-make-wine.net/winemaking/
This is another example and is the exact same platform as the last page. This one is a site on how to make your own wine. Again it's got your lead capture form on it along with articles and additional good stuff. The articles go here - anytime you do any posting it goes here. This one has these tags up here, which are actually links to every individual article, so it publishes those there.

These last two steps I showed you require that you purchase a domain name and a hosting account. By doing this you will have more flexibility and the ability to make a great looking site.

You can go to WordPress.com and learn all about it if you really want to take on a challenge because it is a bit more complex. WordPress has a back end that you log into, and you can put in a statistics plug-in where you can track hits and statistics. They have hundreds of thousands of plug-ins that do all kinds of stuff. WordPress is a much steeper learning curve. When you compare Blogger to Active Rain, there's a world of difference. Active rain is fairly static - you can't do much with it. With Blogger you can move things around and you can add all kinds of things to it. Plus you have the option of changing your background along with lots of different options available for customizing your blog.

WordPress is like blogger on steroids. It is the most versatile blogging platform, there is. You can do a ton of stuff with WordPress. WordPress has something called an all-in-one search engine optimization pack, and if you install that plug-in on WordPress, it does all the things possible to optimize your blog for search engine rankings. It makes it come out ahead of blogger.

If you want to dominate the first page of Google for a listing then I suggest you follow this route:

1.   Set up Blogger

2.   Set up Active Rain

3.   Set up WordPress

You want to have one blog that acts as your main site. This is where you are going to continually post new content. You can place new listings and open houses on it. In addition you can post information about local restaurants, great places to shop along with community news and activities. These sites should be listed on one side of your blog.

It will take some time to get your main page looking the way you want it to, but remember as your site ages Google will visit more often, don't forget to add new content regularly. The longer your site stays active the higher it will get ranked in the search engines. Remember what we said at the beginning about Google owning Blogger? Google loves blogs and the longer yours is around the better for your business.

Recap – When using WordPress dot com it is free but you do need to have a hosting account. One thing you do need to know is how to use Blogger, and add content to it. Learn how to post automatic content coming from MLS to your blog. This information is the most recent and keeps your customers notified of changes as they happen.

Make sure you use a lead capture form and only ask for a name and an email address. Offer something like a free report in exchange, you will be pleasantly surprised by how many people take you up on your offer!

If you are not sure what type of information to offer people for free, just search Google for ideas. Of course you want to offer access to MLS but provide them with information on how to move up to a larger home, how to trade up without moving twice, how to apply for a home loan and even tips on how to avoid the biggest mistakes homebuyers make.

Another good place to look for special reports is the National Association of Realtors. Their website has tons of free information. You can copy and paste them into your site or you could rewrite them a little and add your own special tips to them. Once you have your reports written I suggest you save them into a PDF file to email people. Remember your goal with these reports is to educate and to motivate your potential customers. The action you want to take is for them to call you, so don't forget to suggest this to them and to provide your phone number at the end of each report.

By the way, all these websites I showed you are mine. I've got lots of blogs out there, and they're very inexpensive if you do the hosted version, and they're free if you do the WordPress.com version. Blogger is free and so is Active Rain. Remember if you don't take advantage of that fact someone else will.

Think about this for a minute, what market area do you like to work in? Another Realtor may like the same area and what if that person does all this work, and you don't? Who's going to get the traffic? They're going to start calling that person and not even know who you are. You're going to have to embrace some of this technology. Yes it is going to take time to learn and get set up on your computer. You're going to have to do it, because if you don't do it someone else will and they're going to get the business and you're not.

Here's an Example: There's a large company that went out of business in Las Vegas that had nine offices back in 2007. This 9-office company had 1200 real estate agents. Their solution for their downturn in their market was to advertise more. Their thought was if the numbers of calls are dropping off we need to advertise more. Their solution caused them to go bankrupt.

Their call volume started going down… why did their call volume go down? They all thought it was because the market was slowing. There's more than one reason why the call volume went down during this time, not just in Las Vegas but nation-wide.

The reason was because people were starting to use the Internet more and more to search for all kinds of information, including searching for a new home. People want more information and print ads don't provide this, they are too limited. On the internet you have the ability to provide unlimited information. You can literally give people the scoop on any particular house.

If you want to look at an aerial satellite picture of it, you can access that on the Internet. Can I get that in the newspaper? I'm not saying don't ever advertise in print media. I'm saying that the response rates have dropped off dramatically, and it happened coincidentally at the same time the market slowed down and everybody sat back and went… well it's just a slow market, I'll just keep advertising.

You see two things happened at the same time. The market slowed down and the customers quit going to the print media, and they started looking for everything on the Internet. We all confused that with… well it's just a slow market and that must be the only thing.

Our customers have changed their behavior, and they did it around 2004 to 2008. Most of them are all converted now and have become Internet wizards. They get it and they know how to find anything they want on the Internet. My parents are in their 70's even they get it! The kids have always gotten it. If my parents know how to find stuff on the Internet, and they spend an hour or two a day looking at Cruise Critic, figuring out where they're going to take your next cruise you know they understand and appreciate the internet.

It's time that we as a group, I don't want to offend anybody but, we as a group are an aging population. For those of us that are not in our 20's, we came in on the back end of this Internet thing. We got into our business and figured out our own way of doing things. We figured out a way to generate revenue and the model changed and nobody told us. If you have never read the book "Who Moved My Cheese," then you should. It is exactly what has happened to us. We were going about our business raking in the dough and somebody - our customers just changed what they were doing, and we wondered - where did all the dough go? The customers are looking somewhere else now.

If you don't do anything else with all that you have learned, then at least set up a blog about your real estate business and keep posting your listings to it. This way each new listing will easily be found on page one of Google.

Chapter 6 – Dominating Google

For one listing set up your first free blog for that address. Name the blog the address - put up photos of the house and the description - use different e-mail - set up another blog with a slight variation of the address in the title. The idea is when somebody searches on that address you want all 10 results to be yours. So it doesn't matter what they click on they are going to come to your page with your contact information on. That's the key.

Free Ads

Here is a completely free site www.usfreeads.com where you can place ads. Plus Google loves this site. When you place your ad on usfreeads.com it will show up in Google within 15 minutes on the first page.

The process for setting up each new listing is still the same. Use your WordPress blog, use a Blogger Blog, use Active Rain and add US Free Ads to the mix. When placing an ad here you should use the address of the property as your title and then include a good description about the house and property. Include your contact information and the website address where an interested prospect can go for more information. Remember to tell them to Google the address in your ad!

You can include more information with each ad but this entails using the paid version. At the time of writing it was $5 per month and allows you to add photos to your ads.

Hubpages

www.hubpages.com is another site you can use to put up a free site. You can title it with the address, or you can title it with the subdivision name. Hubpages are just another type of blog. You can still place pictures of the house on there and people are able to leave comments.

Your goal is to generate leads from as many different sources as possible. By providing customers with lots of information they are more likely to trust you and fill out your lead capture forms. Remember to follow up with your leads and answer all their questions in a timely manner. Providing quality customer service is key.

Squidoo

Squidoo is another free hosting site. You set up what is called a Squidoo Lens which again is just another form of a blog. With a Squidoo lens you can put pictures and descriptions of your listings. Don't forget to name the lens with the address of the house.

It is not always possible to add a lead capture form to all of these free sources. If you find one that doesn't allow this then simply add a resource list. This could say something to the effect of:

Check Out My Other Listings

Or

For Further Information Visit My Main Site

By now you have at least six or seven different free sources where you can set up listings. Once you get the hang of setting one up they can be done within minutes.

Something to keep in mind: With all of these blogs you can edit them at any time. This is particularly important once a house is sold. Just edit the listing to show it as sold but the key thing here is not to lose a potential lead. To do this you simply add a note to the effect of Click Here for Similar Listings. This is the perfect way to make use of your traffic and not lose anyone.

Craigslist

This is another place that you can put an ad for your property that will be indexed by Google. Put an ad for each property using the same guidelines as before. Use the address for the title and include a good description of the property.

Chapter 7 - Follow Up – Follow Up

We have talked about generating leads. Now the question becomes once you get a lead what is your next move? The simple answer is to follow up with them. This might sound obvious but it is a fact that gets overlooked. Believe me I know, I've been a realtor for 23 years. I used to suck at follow-up! In fact you can give realtors leads, leads and more leads. What most do is to call them one time and then make assumptions about whether they are buyers or not. You try them one time, and if they're not ready to buy then you're gone. Everyone wants to find that person that is ready to buy right now! This just isn't going to happen. Instead you need to have an automatic system in place that communicates with your customers on your behalf. This system is known as a Contact Management which we will discuss next.

Contact Management

Before you start using social media tools like Facebook, Twitter and auto responders you need to understand the big picture and the importance of how contact management all fits together. I'm going to show you a manual contact management system so you get the picture. Then as you learn the automated tools you'll understand how they fit in with the big picture.

One of the most amazing contact management software programs is Top Producer. When top producer came out, it was six floppy discs you had to load into your computer. If you have seen Top Producer, it's got stuff that's just amazing. Now it has so many toys on it that if you use all the toys you never have any time to sell houses. You don't have time to show houses you're too busy updating your toys. The fact is that 80% of the time on contact management systems is not spent on contact management - it's spent on playing with all the toys and all the bells and whistles. Top Producer has got to the point where they've got so much stuff on it that they're counterproductive, and you don't need that many bells and whistles. You don't have time for contact management systems. You can save your money by not buying expensive software and set up a little analogue version that will be just as effective.

Warm and Fuzzy (WF)

The only things that you need to track are warm fuzzy things. It doesn't matter what their price range is or where they want to live. You have learned from experience that people constantly change their mind on those 2 items. You show them houses in an area, they requested for three days, and then they want to look at another area. You see none of that stuff matters. What matters is the warm fuzzy stuff. When I'm talking about here is:

I care about you

I remember you

I think about you

You have to come up with things that let them know that this is what you really think. These are things you need to pay attention to and track.

Combining Automation and WF

Automating all your contact management with the warm fuzzy things can be difficult because when we're talking about automating things we're talking about letting a machine do it. You too will need to be involved because this is a high touch business. The information you want to get from these people can't all be used for use in your automated follow-up. Your automated follow-up is an extra tool to use to free up some of your time.

For example when you send e-mails you probably type them and you send them saying... "hey, I'm just checking in with you". That takes time and you don't want to have to do that one by one anymore. You have more valuable things to do with your time. You're still going to have to make personal contact with them at points in your follow-up cycle. Whichever method you choose you're still going to have to have a hard copy system to keep you on track and that needs to be as simple as possible.

Hard Copy Contact Management

This is a system that will cost you approximately five bucks. That is much better than paying $500 for a contact management system. Contact management systems have categories of people and the way to use categories is to just have a few say 6 or 7 and then have a lot of people in every category. The biggest category you will have is your past customers and clients. For some new agents, it might be your future customers and clients. Your past customers and clients are gold. Do you follow up with your past customers and clients at least 12 times a year? If you want to retire, you have got to have a book of business and the only way you can have a book of business is if you follow up with every-body you helped buy or sell a home. You follow up with them until you go to their funeral. Then you can stop the follow-up. I'm not kidding. That's how you keep a book of business forev-er.

You want to have a few categories of people... past customers and clients, buyers, prospects, seller prospects, lenders or affiliates would be even broader. Keep these people in an e-mail list and I advise you to keep a hard copy somewhere else. First you need to decide what these categories are going to be. You need four or five primaries. Primaries are people that can make you money and include past customers and clients. Your sec-ondary category is people such as inspectors, lenders, business contacts and friends. These are the people that you actually have to manage. These are the ones you are going to use this warm fuzzy stuff with.

You Do Care

Once you have the broad categories set up - the information that you are going to track is going to be related to things that will make your prospects think you care. Not saying you have to care about them personally but the information you gather from them is going to make them think you care. There's a downside to all this caring, they are going to feel from you. They will think that you are their friend. That can be scary. If they think you are their friend that means when their dog gets away who are they going to call? When they have a little life emergency, they think you're their friend so they're going to call you and tell you all about it. It's good to have friends but the numbers of people that you have got to work through over time will be in the thousands if you're going to make any decent money in this business. Can you imagine 1000 people calling you saying that their car broke down and can you come and help me? You don't want that to happen but believe me it does. On the other hand, you want these people to think that you care because they will continue to refer you and send you more business, which is what you want to happen.

Don't Suck At Follow Up

Following up with prospects is extremely important! If you have one potential customer and you keep in contact by following up it will eventually lead to a sale. Look at it this way, if you have 100 prospects and you never follow up with them your business will be slow. You will do business but it will be more difficult to get this business.

The way to turn the majority of your leads into a customer is to follow up and to automate the process. As a realtor, you need to stay in touch with everyone, not just those that you like. At some point these people will be looking to buy or sell a home and you want to be around when they do.

The Ford System

Here is the Ford system. These are the four pieces of information that you will gather and if you track this and tie it to a prospect… they are going to think you like them. Here's what it stands for:

Family

Organizations

Recreation

Dreams

When you're talking to somebody new, these are the four pieces of information that you want to extract from them. This is not how we do it:

"Hi Bob, Mike Caraway. How are you doing? Nice to meet you. I got a few questions I need to ask you… who's in your family and what do you do for fun?"

That is not going to work. But it is really easy if you're just standing around talking to people in casual conversation.

This is how you do it:

"Hey Bob. What are you doing here today, are you getting any useful information out of this program? Oh yeah, where are you from? Hoover, is that where your families from? Have you got a lot of family in Hoover? So you're from there, you grew up there? You go to church there? Oh in Alpha Deana okay. Are you a member of any organizations or clubs? You got any kids?"

A lot of people will really elaborate on the kids questions. Some will give you all their names and ages. All you have to do once you get them going is… **Shut Up**. You shut up and let them talk because once you get them going they will tell you everything you want to know about them and their family.

The hard part is making mental notes and remembering what they are telling you while you are in that initial encounter. You have to make mental notes because if you can walk away from that little chance encounter and immediately write that stuff down, you've got a good contact there. When you call them or e-mail them the next time you can mention their kids. Hope the kids, Bobby and Timmy are doing okay, and they are thinking - "wow that person remembered me. They cared enough to remember my kid's names." If they talked about any of their dreams that they want to do one day you can refer to these goals and talk about them.

These four topics will tend to make people think you really care about them, you're impressed with them, you like them, and they want to talk to people who like them, it just part of human nature. When you run into someone and say "I remember you from _____," their teeth will show because they are smiling. Therefore, if you can remember things about people, they really like that. But you can't remember this about hundreds of people you have to write it down.

Organizing That Information

Once you get this information you need to record it in some sort of fashion that's organized. This way it can be easily referenced and also put it in some kind of a follow-up system.

This brings us back to that $5 hard copy contact information system that was mentioned. All you need to use is a 4 x 6 index card for each person you are working with. They sell these little file boxes at stationary stores for a couple of dollars and it will hold about 1000 of those cards. What you need to do is write down some fields just like any contact management system would have. Unlike paid contact management systems, you only need a small amount of fields to make this work. Here are the required fields you will need:

Name

Phone

Address

Email

Family

Organizations

Recreation

Dreams

This is all the information you need. Get that little file box and then get 30 index tabs and number them 1 to 30. Write these fields down on those 4 x 6 index cards. That's all you need, that's it. That's our contact management system. You just need 1 through 30 on the little tabs because those are the days of the month, and it doesn't matter what month were in, it always works.

Chapter 8 – Action Plan

Now that you have your contact management system ready which is simply your file box filled with index cards. There are certain steps that should occur with every contact in a certain category. Remember you only need about 6 or 7 categories. So how many action plans do we need? The action plan includes letters, postcards, phone calls, visits, e-mails, tweets, broadcast. It includes all the stuff we are going to do to this person over time.

Some of these things, until they invent robots, you are going to have to do yourself. Wouldn't it be nice if we could get letters, postcards, of course phone calls, e-mails, tweets, broadcasts, all of it to happen automatically? That's where you are headed after you understand how this all fits together. This can be applied to whatever prospect you want to apply it to. With this action plan, once you have categorized that person automatically you know what action plan they fit into.

Do you think it might be a good idea to stay in touch with customers? If you do, you will be the only one doing it right now. Very few people do that. If they hear of somebody wanting to buy or sell a house, who are they going to give the referral too, especially since you are the one following up with them, and staying in touch with them? They are going to call you or recommend you because you're the only one following up.

Here's an example of an action plan. This is the number of days between activities.

Day	Activity
0	Thank you Note
3	Phone Call 1
4	Letter 1
4	Postcard 1
1	Email 1
4	Phone Call 2
5	Letter 2
3	Email 2
4	Phone Call 3
6	Letter 3
4	Email 3

You will have a thank you note going out, a phone call, a letter, a postcard, an e-mail, phone call 2, letter 2, e-mail 2, phone call

3, letter 3, and e-mail 3. The basic follow-up sequence is call, mail, call, mail, call and mail. We also have other things to use to in our arsenal. Now we have e-mails and we could also use a face book group broadcast. We got some other things that we can throw into this mix instead of just call mail, call mail, call and mail. We can hit them from more angles... it's more interesting that way to them.

Letter1.doc

For this example to work well you want to type up a basic letter and save it into a folder. This letter doesn't have to be long. It is more of a reminder to them that you are still around and available. As you get more leads you may want to set this letter up as a template. You can then use a mail merge feature to personalize each letter effortlessly. You are essentially creating your own database.

David Knox has some excellent training guides you can consider looking at. He has a whole video on prospecting and his whole spin on it is... have you ever bought something from a bad salesperson? Why, because they were the only ones there. Even if you're bad, if you're there enough you're going to get business. If you're going to personalize these letters and do mail merge, then that warm fuzzy stuff is what really makes it work and blows them away.

Letter 1 Sample -

Hi Bob,

It was great talking with you the other day. I look forward to helping you and____ find the home that's perfect for you. Now is a great time to buy, because the rates are so low. By the way, how's it going with Frisbee golf and your dog? (Just add some of that warm fuzzy personal stuff that you found out about them through your last conversation.)

Give me a call when something great happens.

Sincerely,

This is not a good letter, but it will do. The whole point is you have to contact these people and touch them on a personal level.

Phone Call 1 Sample -

Hey Bob, what's up? This is Mike. We talked yesterday at the sewage treatment plant. I just wanted to give you a quick call to let you know I haven't forgotten about you and ____ so I've already put together some homes you may want to take a look at.

If you script these things out, then you don't have to worry about what you are going to say when you call them… because the not knowing what to say, is what will keep you from picking up the phone and calling. Create a short phone script to follow up with these people and write it down. Type it up and save it as phonecall1.doc and put it in a buyer follow-up folder on your desktop.

Email 1 Sample –

I just got some information on home loans, and that I thought you would be interested in it. Since you and _____ are eager. I wanted to be sure I kept you as up to date as possible. By the way, I met someone yesterday who is interested in _____ too!

Save your letters, your phone scripts into a file on your desktop called ___, whatever the category is. Remember you only have seven categories so you only need seven folders. Create a folder called buyers, a folder called sellers, a folder called past clients, a folder called affiliates etc and put the follow-up information that you created in them.

Most people don't do this because you have to do something to make it work. Yes, you have to sit down and actually produce some letters and phone calls scripts. Just sit down and make time to get these letters created. Remember it's not necessarily what you say that is important as much as the fact that you are saying something to them. Just make sure it conversational as if they were standing in front of you.

Look at your Action Plan

You have met somebody new… Bob tells you that he's thinking about buying a house in the next six months. The normal agent inside your head says, "I'm not talking to him, I'm not waiting six months." You're going to stay in touch with him for six months. This is really easy because now all I need is some of that warm fuzzy stuff. Make friends with Bob and remember this warm fuzzy stuff he told you. I might say… Hey Bob listen, I'm going to get information on houses from time to time, do you mind if I just drop it in the mail to you? I don't want to bother you.

I'm going to take down his information. Then go back and put it on a little card and put him in my home buyer follow-up plan. Then you look at your action plan and do the first activity. For example, if it was a little thank you note I just drop him a note in the mail. I'm going to do the first activity and then if it says the next activity is four days from now and today is the fourth I'm going to take that card and stick it in on the eighth. When it becomes the eighth, I am going to pull his card out and say it's time for activity number two. All I have to do is look at his category and see that I've already done step one on the action plan. I'll look at his category and know what the next step is. I do that next step whatever it is, a phone call or an e-mail, or a letter, and then it says the next activity is three days later, so I move it three days back. See how this is automatic? In doing it this way you can handle thousands of people in many different categories. Do the activity, and then move it back the number of days in your little file box. If today is the 30th, and I'm supposed to get in touch with him and do the next activity on the four days later it's going to be the fourth, so I put it in the fourth. I'm always just looking at today's date.

When you start each day look in your file box at what you have to do today. Go into today's date and pull out your whole stack of cards. Some of them are buyer prospects, some of them are for sale by owners, some of them are past clients that I need to do an action for. You sit down and do your follow-up work. It's that easy. You don't have to wonder about what you're supposed to do that day or who you're supposed to call. This will not work, unless you set this stuff up in advance. You have to set up your action plans and populate them with content. This is exactly how all that high fangled software works except it's the analog version, and it only costs a few dollars. Your action plan will control your activities. You don't have to wonder what you're going to send them… you've already created that.

A lot of businesses fret over how their ad pieces look, and they'll delay a product launch because of that. Meanwhile nobody's buying the product, because they don't have anything out there. It's better to do something now, then do nothing or fret about how it's going to look. The little file boxes can handle a thousand people that way in all seven different categories. They will all think that you are paying personal attention to them.

Chapter 9 – Automating Your Process

Automate your follow-up e-mail

One of the things we can automate in this sequence is the e-mail. You would never have to send another prospect an e-mail, unless they directly asked you something. In other words, you're going to be following up with them every three or four days by e-mail, but you're not.

There is another free tool available that you can use as an auto responder. Most auto responders cost money, or they put ads in your e-mail. Now, as much as I want to be there, I don't want to have an ad for how to grow hair on my head in my e-mail that I'm sending to a customer or a prospective client. It is called www.freeautobot.com. When you go to their website it has all kinds of ads everywhere that they use as their revenue model. It will have pop-ups and stuff, so just wait until they all come up and close them all. Then you can set up a free account. Put in your e-mail address and your details and then you can start setting up your e-mails.

You need to have an understanding of what an auto responder is and how it works. Remember earlier when you learned about the lead capture form? The auto responder allows you to add leads manually. You can go in and type in their name and e-mail address and hit enter and the people will start getting your sequence of e-mails. Basically, the lead capture form does the same thing. When they click on submit it goes to the auto responder, which sends them your first e-mail in your sequence.

I meet Bob and we're checking out cantaloupes… I ask him how to tell if these are ripe or not… he says, you just have to feel them. What do you feel for? We talk about cantaloupes, and then the conversation turns into looking for a house. Somehow you have to get the conversation to real estate. A tidbit - If you haven't thought about hanging out in a grocery store by the fruits and vegetables section looking for leads you should! It really does work.

Back to Bob and the conversation which has been turned into real estate by you. You get their information and take it back and add him to your auto responder so that he gets the e-mails in the right sequence. It's going to be integrated with my action plan. Remember it doesn't cost anything to do this, it's free. Plus you can have unlimited accounts if necessary. You need just seven because you have seven categories of people. You set up seven accounts on free autobot, they will all require a different username and password. Make a note of these so you can easily access your accounts at any time.

When using a free autoresponder service the delivery rate of your emails may not be the best. It is possible that after someone fills out your form they won't receive the next message for a day or two. This is just something to be aware of.

There's paid auto responders that are awesome. Most paid auto responders cost about $20 a month. A couple of very good paid auto responders are Get Response and Aweber. **http://www.Aweber.com/?303301** A favorite of many business owners is Aweber. It has statistics, you can tell when a customer opens an e-mail, and you can tell when they click on something in the e-mail. It has all kinds of these great features. It has a lot of customized features. You can put pictures in your e-mail, and you can put attachments on it.

Let's understand what this auto responder thing is. It is the pre-programmed sequence of e-mails that your prospect will receive directly from you, and it can be personalized so it says:

Hi Jane,

This is Shannon again. I just wanted to drop you a quick e-mail to let you know I haven't forgotten about you. You might be interested to know that there are a lot of things happening in the real estate market right now. Call me to find out what they are, or call me if you have any questions.

Great talking to you again,

Shannon

You don't need anything that is long and drawn out. You don't have to send them a 15-page report. You just want to touch base and that's it, it is all very personal. If they reply to it the email will go back to your inbox. See how well that works, they don't know it's automatic, and they don't know that you typed it six months ago. They don't know that you just put this little thing in it that will drop in their first name. They don't have to know any of that stuff… they think it's a real e-mail from you.

Set up Account and Login

Freeautobot.com

This is what you will see after you have signed up and logged this is what you will see. This particular account has 68 leads in it.

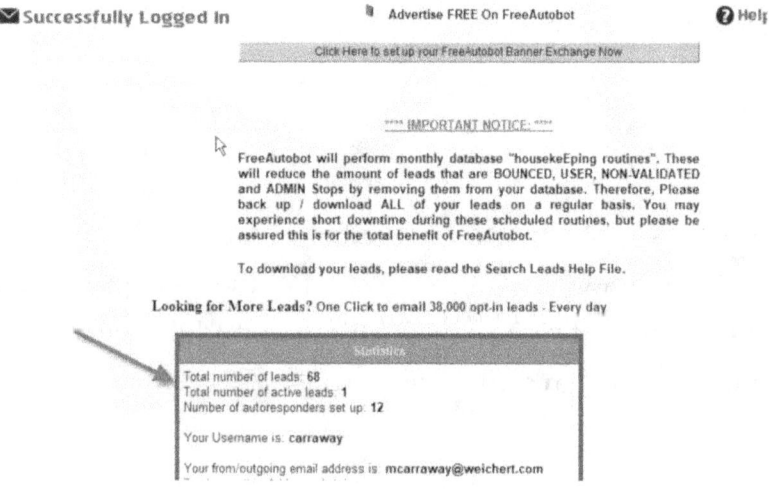

It shows you how many leads you have and how many e-mail follow-ups you have. What you need to do in your e-mail follow-up sequence is space them closer together at the beginning, three or four days apart and then space them out after you get out to about seven e-mails space them out to about six or seven days apart and then about 10 days apart.

Once you're in this... you want to click on message control... this will take you to the messages.

The first thing I want to show you is where it says help. This is where the magic comes in. You copy and paste all this code into your JavaScript HTML box. There are a couple of things in red. Username is whatever your username is that you set this account up with. Mine is Carraway for this account, so I would put Carraway in there. This says success URL... that's the web page they go to after they submit their name and e-mail. You don't want them to leave your page, so just put your web page in there... your blog address. If someone fills out the form on your blog, and they click submit it will just keep them on the same page and not take them into cyberspace. It's important that you keep your customers on the same page after they have submitted their name and e-mail address. Copy this whole thing and paste it into your HTML Java box. When you do that... you will have a little form that says enter your name and e-mail address. When they enter it and click submit their going to instantly get the first e-mail that you have in here.

ALSO. You can include an "Add Lead / Opt-In" form on your site, allowing visitors to Add themselves (Opt-In) and receive your FreeAutoBot messages. Copy and paste the following HTML code to the source (raw HTML) within your page.

```
<!---START OF ADD FORM-->
For more information please fill out this form <br><br>
<form action="http://freeautobot.com/cgi-bin/autores/autores.cgi">
<input type=hidden name="do" value="add_lead_external">
<input type=hidden name="Username" value="USERNAME">
<input type=hidden name="Stop_Status" value="Active">
<input type=hidden name="Cycle_Number" value="0">
<input type=hidden name="Success_URL" value="http://freeautobot.com">
<input type=hidden name="Failure_URL" value="http://freeautobot.com/Failure.html">
<input type=hidden name="Notes" value="Added from opt-in form">
Name: <input type=text name="Name" value=""><br>
Email Address: <input type=text name="Email" value=""><br>
<input type=submit value="Submit">
</form>
<!---END OF ADD FORM-->
```

Please edit the two fields shown in red above to reflect your own site.
Replace USERNAME with your FreeAutoBot Username

If you want your prospect to go to another page after they have submitted your Opt-In Form, replace http://freeautobot.com with your own URL details. Enter this under the

Layout is Key

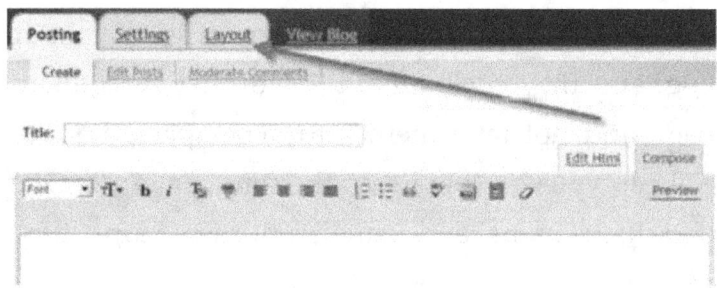

This is the control panel in blogger.com. You will go to the layout tab and in there you are going to click on add a gadget or add a page element.

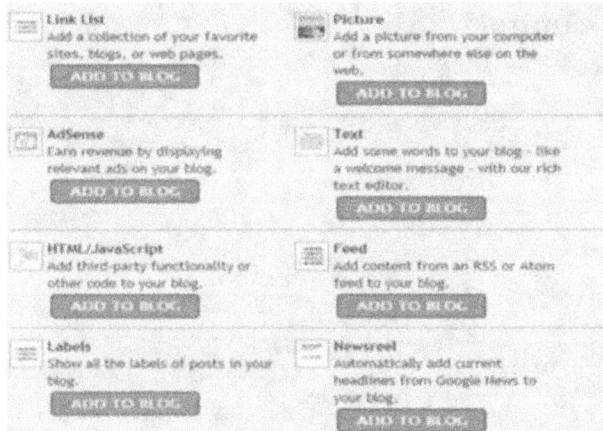

This page will come up, and you'll want to go to use the HTML JavaScript gadget.

You paste the code from above inside this box.

After pasting that code into here you click save. Now you have a form on your blog that people can fill in their name and e-mail address.

Message Control

[CLICK HERE to edit your double opt-in confirmation email or LEAVE BLANK for our default message]

Message #	Subject	Send	Status	Edit	Delete
0	Your FREE Special Real Estate Report	0	To Deactivate this message click here	Edit	☐
1	Is it time to buy a new home?	4	To Deactivate this message click here	Edit	☐
2	6 Mistakes to Avoid when Buying a home	5	To Deactivate this message click here	Edit	☐
3	Are you still interested in buying a home?	8	To Deactivate this message click here	Edit	☐
4	How to save Thousands when you buy a home - FREE REPORT	7	To Deactivate this message click here	Edit	☐
5	We have a wonderful 3 br. 2 bath home for you!	6	To Deactivate this message click here	Edit	☐
6	get an extra $4,000 when you sell your home	10	To Deactivate this message click here	Edit	☐
7	Mortgages are SCARY!	10	To Deactivate this message click here	Edit	☐

Back on freeautobot.com you can see the actual letter sequence that I have. Message number zero is the e-mail they are going to get as soon as they click submit. This is that free special real estate report that was promised to them. That's what will be in the subject line. If I was offering them a free special real estate report on my website or blog, and they filled in their name and e-mail and clicked submit... they are going to get this e-mail instantly. Sometimes it can take longer depending on the traffic on the auto responder. That's why it is recommended to have a paid version, but this will work. The Send tab is the number of days between each e-mail. If they were to get this one today, which is the fourth then 10 days later they're going to get this one, which is the 14th. This is amazingly set up just like your action plan is set up. If you have an e-mail in your action plan going out your prospect at certain intervals, you can set it up that way on this. You are integrating your automatic e-mails with your action plan.

Recap – Inside your account, your message control area is where you can see all your email messages. This is all part of the system which you did with those index cards. You had to set up your action plan and then plan and create the content. Creating letters and phone scripts was done in advance. You are doing the same thing here with your email messages, creating and setting them up in advance inside an autoresponder system. As you get a new contact you can add them into your account and their emails go out automatically.

They're going to get the e-mails automatically according to your follow-up action plan schedule. So my first e-mail, you don't want them to get it for 12 days. It's going to send one automatically as soon as you put them in so there will be an extra e-mail right there. Then my next e-mail is going to go out 12 days later. I'm going to go ahead and compose that e-mail and save it in my auto responder, which is freeautobot.com. Then at 12 days later you are going to have another one go out. You only need to it up one time, and when you get a new prospect you enter them in there, and they are going to get the e-mails automatically.

Remember realtors suck at follow-up, so if you blow off all the rest of this, they will at least get an e-mail from you. This allows them to remember your name and what you do!

Use the HELP file to Personalize

Here's the good thing about this particular auto responder... you can actually use these little tags to help personalize your emails.

<%Email%>

<%First_Name%>

<%Last_Name%>

<%Name%>

You can copy and paste where you want their first name to go. If they fill out the form, and they put Bobby as their name, and Bobby@yahoo.com as their e-mail, instead of having to put Bobby in the letter or the e-mail yourself all you do is just copy and paste this <%First_Name%> every place you want it to say that person's name. You copy and paste that in there and before that e-mail goes out it's actually mail merged with his name and then that e-mail goes out automatically, and it's personalized for Bobby and Bobby thinks you sent it personally to him.

If you know someone is not interested in buying a house for six months, then you need six months worth of e-mail follow-ups. Yes it will it take some time to sit down and create all those e-mails. When you do you will want to think about it because good part is you only have to do it one time.

You can start out using the free auto responder, but eventually you may want to upgrade to a paid version. Besides, all the fancy things, you can do with the paid versions, the best part is being able to include an attachment. Being able to send a video to a client of the inside of a house that they are interested is well worth the monthly fee of the paid versions.

Use your smart phone

Another tool that is being used now-a-days is your cell phone, and they too can be integrated into this whole process. The big thing is if you have a phone that is e-mail enabled, not only can you send e-mail and text message, you've also got a database with customizable fields for every entry you make into your phone.

When you add a contact it has fields to put their name, address phone numbers, e-mail address. If you scroll down from there you will see customizable fields at the bottom, and you can call those, whatever you want. In that spot, there are 4 things you need... remember the FORD system. You need family, organizations, recreation and dreams. A lot of people are not very good with names and when I see somebody in the grocery store, and they come walking up to me, I'm panicking because I know I sold them a house. I don't remember their name - I just remember the face. I might remember a few things about them like, they've got a dog named Skip.

Now if I have done everything I am supposed thus far then I've already put in family, organizations, recreation and dreams so I should be able to search on Skip because your phone has a find feature, and it will look through all that stuff and it will find that person. So if you are really good then you can say "hold on, I'm on call, or I've got to send a text" and then you search really fast and find them. Then you can say, hey what's going on Becky, good to see you again. If you just can't for the life of you remember their name, and you have all their personal information in your phone, you can search on a clue. That's an easy way to use this, and they'll think you're smart. Just put them in your phone but add those little tags that you can search on. That will make you seem like a realtor that can remember people's names.

Some phones have find, and some phones search - it just depends on what kind of phone you have. I can search if I remember the person's hobby is kite building or basket weaving or anything I can remember about that person.

Something to keep in mind - I hope you are getting all this and putting it into action because if you didn't you're going to start falling behind.

Past Clients = Future Revenue

This is a lesson you don't want to learn the hard way, like I did. This is why the most important category of people is past customers and clients. I captured a lead and I followed up with the guy. He even actually called me and said he needed me to come help him sell his house. I did sell his house, and I helped him and his family buy another house. I also helped his daughter get a house, and that all happened within nine months. We were in contact the whole time.

Two years later, I was sitting at a restaurant having dinner with my wife, and I see this guy at this table and I knew I knew them but I couldn't remember his name for the life of me. He saw me and asked if I was still in the real estate business. I said, of course I am. He said he wished he had of known that because he sold that house and his daughter sold her house and they all bought new houses. Lack of follow-up cost me about $16,000, and it would've cost me about five dollars a year for those two years to stay in touch with him.

That's why following up is important, if you are following up and no business is produced that's okay. In time you will generate business from this system which you now have in place. The person you are following up with may not need a realtor but one of their friends may ask for a referral. Who are they going to recommend? Obviously you because you were following up with them all this time. All you need do is keep in touch with them around 12 to 36 times in a year. You automate the process so it doesn't take you any extra time at all, only the time and effort it cost to set it up in the first place.

By the way, you can send them the same stuff every year because they will forget. They won't know it's January, and I'm waiting for that one e-mail that I always get every January.

That's not going to happen they're going to forget what you're sending them from year to year. Maybe after 10 years they'll start catching on. Basically, you can send these people the same old stuff as long as you're staying in touch with them, and you only have to call them about once every two months just to touch base. Your action plan for your past clients has to be 12 months long, but you can just repeat it. You just keep doing it over and over. This is definitely the most important category you've got, and you cannot and I mean cannot forget about that one, that's the most important one.

A lot of people that get in this business, make a sale and then say, whew, I'm glad I'm done with those people. I am so glad I don't have to talk to them anymore. Well, those are the people you want to talk to. They've already had an experience with you - they've already undergone your personal service, they know what to expect, and they know what their friends can expect from you. Those are the people you've got to stay in touch with. If you make them angry, and they close and they didn't talk to you at the closing table you do not have to put them in your follow-up program. It's not going to help you.

Past Clients

They deserve their own category, their own action plan that repeats every year. You have to call these people, and I would say at least six times a year. They should be your number one e-mail list - your number one follow-up. If you are going to put something in the auto responder, and you don't do anything else… put your past customer follow-up in there. The purpose of your e-mail is to really say "Hi, I am still here."

Automatically Email New Listings

The prospect search in MLS is another automatic function that once you set it up you can forget it. You need to use this to send out new listings that match your prospects interests. If you're not using this you need to go to learn how it works. There are help files on MLS to show you how to do it. It is an automatic feature that will free your time up will not have to search but one time for every prospect. Then they automatically get new listings via e-mail. You are contacting them and they don't know it's a machine. That's the beautiful thing… They have no idea you automated this feature and don't tell them. Don't devalue the service because you pay for it. It cost you $30 a month for this feature, so use it and make sure that they know you're doing the work.

Chapter 10 – Twitter

That's the new buzzword in the media. This can add something to your follow-up, and it also allows you another way to capture leads and prospects. One of the new up-and-coming applications that are out there, it's actually been around since 2006 believe it or not... Twitter. Twitter can be a little tough to figure out how to use it because in its entirety it can it seem like a bunch of noise. There are tools out there that you can benefit from, and you will learn the benefits, but you first have to know where these tools are. With Twitter, you can get on there and type in a bunch of stuff in every now and then, but you don't know who reads it so it can seem sort of worthless.

Then there is Facebook... Facebook has recently enjoyed a large surge in popularity from people over 35 years of age. People are always asking if you are on Facebook. Facebook used to be a school kids deal, but not anymore. You put your profile up on Facebook with your name on it, and you'll have people that you went to high school with sending you friend requests tomorrow.

They did a segment on 60 Minutes about Facebook and put a profile up for Leslie Stahl. Right after she was set up with a Facebook profile, she got a friend request from somebody she went to high school with... that quick. People will find you may not want everybody finding you. Part of this social networking gig is trying to figure out how to get rid of the noise and boil it down to things that we can use to make money. The problem is you can't seem like you're there just to make money. Remember it has to be all about the conversation and the warm fuzzy I care about you. You've got to build a relationship with these people before you can turn them into a potential customer. If they don't trust you based on the content you have on your Facebook site, or what you're sending them on Twitter, they're never going to work with you. It has to be conversational in nature.

Twitter.com

When you type in www.twitter.com, this is the main page.

All you have to do is sign up and it's free.

You do need to create a username and this takes a little thinking about first. It will be the name that you are recognized on all over Twitter, so it should be connected to your business. Something like RLTR4U what do you think most people would think that said? Realtor for you... that's too salesy... don't use it. It is probably not available anyway. You want something about real estate for a username. You do want people to know that you're in the real estate business. When you come up with a user name you know it is going to be put out there publicly, and you want people to know that you've got something to do with real estate. Houses Are For Me... I wouldn't put - Sold One... that's selling. You don't want something that hints at selling. You want something that is more social, but it also indicates or has an indication of some sort that you are about real estate.

You can set up different Twitter accounts as long as you have different e-mail addresses. You can actually segment the traffic that you are going to get from Twitter into different topic areas. I've got a site on how to make your own homemade wine. It just says wine for you as my username. That username tells people what it is about. People will assume this guy must be into making wine or drinking wine or something about wine. If I had realtor4you as a username then people would know I was into real estate.

The limitations on this - what are you doing is only 140 characters long including spaces so you can't put a whole lot of content in there.

It's very short little e-mails, and it's hard to communicate that way. If you get a new listing, you can put - just listed this house for this much money - and then a link to your website. Then put your website address or your blog address, so they can go take a look at it if they wanted to.

What you want to try to do on Twitter is to get close to 5000 followers, but that takes a long time. The way you do it is by following other people. You find about 200 people, and you have to click on follow. When you click on follow, they have to accept and follow you back. It's kind of like a friend request, but it's quicker. Once you have about 200 people you are following... people are going to start finding your picture and your username, and they are going to start following you. What you're looking for is that social networking thing to start taking hold on its own and mushrooming. I got about five more people following me every day once I got past 200. My number of followers keeps going up, and I've got a little tool set up that automatically re-follows them back so I don't have to go in and do it manually.

It's just like a friend request on Facebook. For those of you who are not YET on Facebook… you can send friend requests to somebody, and they actually have to look at it and click on it to accept you as your friend. On Twitter, it's the same thing but there's a tool that automates it so it will automatically follow people back.

Google finally got wise to this Twitter thing and realized a lot of people were using it. I've got 548 people following me, and every time they type in something that is 140 characters long it pops up down here. It's like noise all the time it's constant ongoing. People from all over just typing in something saying I'm frying eggs right now enter, I'm cleaning my glasses enter, I'm vacuuming, doing the Hoover thing enter. That noise is going on all the time so how do you make sense of all that?

Google's New Application

Like I said, Google finally got it. Google now has an application that will allow you to do a real-time search on Twitter. So now you can start searching for what people are saying, which means you can find people that are house shopping. You can find people that are trying to fix their house up to sell it. Type in - trying to fix my house up to sell it – enter… working on my landscaping hope to sell soon - enter. This is what the Twitter search looks like.

It's the Google application, and it's called Twitter search.

We can type in - house shopping... because that's what customers say they are doing. What are you doing today? We're going house shopping. I typed in house shopping and there are several hits about who is house shopping... Started house shopping - just finished off a bit of house shopping with my broker - is house shopping in LA. These people have recently entered the fact that they were house shopping. You won't know where these people are until you click on any of these

Did you mean: *home* shopping

Twitter / Whitney Hoffman: @kimwood- **house shopping** f...
Twitter is a free social messaging utility for staying connected in real-time.
twitter.com/LDpodcast/statuses/1245101151

Twitter / LP McFall: Started **house shopping** Is...
Started **house shopping** Is now a good time to be looking in the midwest?I'm thinking I'd
rather buy on the way up than on the way down still.9:03 AM Feb 16th ...
https //twitter.com/Ruanon/status/1215840979

taylorphinney: Just finished a bit off **house shopping** with my bro ...
taylorphinney: Just finished a bit off **house shopping** with my bro Scott. At Proto's now...best
Pizza in the USA!
twitter.com/taylorphinney/statuses/1096202206

gchahal: is **house shopping** in LA...
gchahal: is **house shopping** in LA...
twitter.com/gchahal/statuses/1103902146

and it will take you right to their page. Started house shopping - Is now a good time to be looking in the Midwest? I am thinking I would rather buy on the way up then on the way down still. You can click on the picture of the person and follow him and then whatever he types in the Twitter, I'll get to look at them. You can actually target who you want to follow and who you want to be friends with. This is very big... because now it's not just noise.

You can do searches every day and see who's looking to fix up their house to sell. You can see who's wondering what their house value is worth. People type stuff like that into Twitter every day. You can find these people, and if you can't do anything else because they may be out of your area... you can certainly do a referral.

If you want to e-mail him directly... you can put that ampersand @ sign in front of your message and go into Twitter, and send a message, directly to him. It's called a direct message, and only he will get it. You could send him a message saying "hey, where are you looking in the Midwest, I'm a realtor, I can help you." Maybe he will write you back. What you really want him to do is go to your website so you can capture all his information or at least get his e-mail.

Now you have a way to take the noise out of Twitter. Just following the people - which will to take you longer... that is true. But you're going to be following people now and looking at their messages, and they are going to be sending messages all the time. People get hooked on this thing. It can be a bunch of noise, unless you can filter out the noise and find the people you want to read their messages. You can follow buyers!

Key to Twitter

The key to Twitter is to search for home buyers. If you type in home buyers you won't get any results. You are going to have to type in what other people are typing in. Such as - we are thinking about buying a house - thinking about buying - enter. Go to that Google application and find people that would be typing in things that buyers would type in. You have to think of things that sellers would put in. What you might want to do is type in your city or area, and follow everybody that is in your area. Then you have localized it to your market. Go to the person who made the post, click on their profile and then follow them. There's a little button there that says follow... that's how easy it is, and it will say you are now following... whoever.

Whenever they type something into Twitter it comes up on your screen. You can also get all your Twitter tweets to come to your cell phone. If you're following 550 people I don't recommend that because all you'll get is constant text messages from this website.

Tweetlater.com

There is a tool that makes this easy and it's called Tweetlater and is an application. We went through how an auto responder works… it automatically delivers a series of e-mail messages spaced over time like you want them. Tweetlater works like an auto responder for Twitter. If we want to send out a series of messages to everybody that follows you, you can set that up. This is a free application, and you have to set up an account, putting in your Twitter username and a password in there.

This is the application that will automatically follow people back if they decide to follow you, and you don't have to do anything so you can increase your sphere of influence. The only people that can see what you're typing into Twitter are the people following you. It's not really going to work for you if you've only got three people following you. You will have to get more than that. That is why you want to do the search first to find buyers and sellers. Remember, type in things they would type in. That is going to take you a week or two to find the right number of people. Once you get up to 200 it will start taking off by itself.

You want to go into Tweetlater and set up some automatic tweets to send to these people. Every time somebody new signs up, they will get a series of messages from you over time. Then you can forget about this except when you get a new listing. Once again, the automatic tweets you send them have to be conversational in nature. Not… "hey, I've got a house to sell want to buy one?" That's not going to work. Catching Internet leads is like trying to catch flies with chopsticks. If they see you coming, they are out of there, which is why you really have to make it conversational.

People would rather fill out forms then talk to somebody that they don't know, like or trust. You have to build that up in your first few messages you're going to send them. Later on, you can say, "I got this new listing, I just put on the market, you might want to check it out it's here." That will go out to all 450 people that are following you. Some of them are actually going to click on it and go look at it. You got to let them inside a little bit. You've got to tell them a little bit about yourself. I'm making chicken and dumplings tonight, some of the noise you have to put some of that out there to.

Tweetlater you can set up messages in advance. You can also set up what are called direct messages. The direct message is a mail that goes out, and it actually shows up in their e-mail too. It goes directly to that person. So if a new person follows you, they will automatically get a direct set of messages from you over time spaced out. These are almost like direct e-mails. A lot of the Twitter functions, if you use Tweetlater can be automated. You set everything up in advance, and you forget about it.

You're going to have to use the Google Twitter search to find the right people to follow. That's all-important because those are going to be prospects who are thinking of buying, selling, relocating or something related to real estate. You have to think of things that they will type into Twitter like that one example we saw where they typed in - we've been house shopping. You have to think of things that home buyers and home sellers would say when they are trying to tell their buddies what's going on.

Once again, set up an account on Twitter and go to Tweetlater. It's got a lot of functions and there's just too many to cover here. The most important ones are setting up automatic messaging to your new people. That's going to give you a whole other group of possible contacts that could turn into customers, and you can automate the whole thing using Tweetlater. Twitter has 60 million users worldwide. There are a lot of real estate agents on there.

Chapter 11 – Facebook

Facebook.com

You have learned how to use Twitter to start generating leads and how to automate your contact management on Twitter. Now we will look at how you can benefit using Facebook. Obviously, what you want to do is to get your Twitter people to one of your lead capture pages. This allows you to find out more about them and turn them into a real lead using your automated follow-up system. Facebook is getting really popular. I am starting to get friend requests from realtors all over the States. Once again, Facebook is another free avenue that you can use. Facebook is free advertising. You can go on there and put real estate pictures on your page.

You don't want to just go on there and put a bunch of pictures of your listings. People as always are into conversations. They want to see pictures of you, especially your old buddies, which are not really the ones you want to talk to, but it's going to happen. You're going to hear from people you haven't heard from since high school that you may not even remember. They will send a friend request, and you are going to scratch your head trying to figure out who they are. Accept them… you never know where they are, and if they will ever need an agent.

The real advantage about Facebook is you can quickly locate people and business contacts. That's the upside. The downside is it's too dang fun playing with it. That's the bad part about Facebook, once you get on there, you can throw beads at people, tattoo somebody's website… you can do all kinds of silly fun stuff. Don't get hung up on that fun stuff because your time is valuable.

Set up Facebook Groups

You want to do it to enhance your business and make money so let me give you the key. This is the inside scoop on how to control Facebook, and it has to do with groups. You can set up as many groups as you want to, and you control them. The best part is you can e-mail everybody in your group all at one time. You can have several groups and all you have to do, is compose an e-mail and everybody in that group receives your e-mail. Remember don't try to sell them anything they aren't going to buy. What you want to do is be informational and conversational. Groups allow you to segment your market. You can get people to join your group by writing stuff on what is called their wall. It's kind of like a Twitter wall… it's just people putting comments. Some examples of groups, you might want to set up are… first-time home buyers in your area - how to buy a home - how to get the best home loan.

Groups

If I put a group name out there you can send up to 5000 messages. If you have more than 5000 people in your group Facebook will ban you. Keep the number of people in your group below 5000, well below 5000. In fact, when you're just starting out you're going to have a hard time just getting 20 people in there so don't worry about the 5000 limit for now.

This is an e-mail broadcaster tool, and you do not have to be friends with these people. They can just join your group, and you won't even know who they are but you can e-mail them. This gives you a way to make contact with these people, and they can e-mail you back. It is free and the key is all in how you name your group.

You can do searches on Facebook for groups in your own area. There are lots of people who join those groups, and you can join those groups too. They don't know you're a realtor… yet. Create your own group in Facebook. Title your group as a benefit to the person searching. For example, "quick home fix-up's for fast sale." If somebody is searching for group names, and they see that, and they're thinking about selling their house… they might want to join your group. What you have to have is the benefit to being a member of the group in the group name. That's the whole key otherwise people won't join it. If you call it, Bob's group... you're going to be the only one in that group.

What you will do is set up this group, and you put some content in there. Put some quick and easy fix up content in there and as people join the group you can send out a little broadcast to that group every now and then - here's another quick easy fix up to sell your home quicker and faster. Of course you're going to put your contact information at the bottom of it. If you just wait for people to join your group, and you don't do anything, it will take a long time. You have to go out and do friend requests. You're going to have to "friend" people. What that means is… you find somebody, and you click on their picture and say send a friend request. You know what… they don't know who you are because they can't remember the people they went to high school with either, so they're going to accept your friend request. Then you can go to their profile page, and you can type right onto it. "Hey Bob might want to check this out if you're interested in selling your home… it's a group about quick easy fix ups for selling your home… click here. That's all you have to do, and if they're thinking about selling their home they will join that.

You have to go through a lot of people to make this work. Remember with Twitter… how you need to have about 200 people following you before it takes off? Facebook works on that same critical mass principle. People start following you all the time. It's kind of like priming the pump. You've got to get something going first.

Now you don't have to be friends with everybody that's in your group. That's the beauty of groups. You can also have as many groups as you want. Make up content that you think buyers and sellers of houses would like to know about and form a group. It's that easy. You might want to put your city or area on there, otherwise you're going to get people from all over the world trying to find your quick and easy fix ups to sell your house. You want to target it to buyers and sellers in your own area although you can always send out referrals if you get them from other parts of the country. Remember to include the benefit of joining the group in the group name. You're much more likely to get random group joiners that way. Of course, once they join your group you can send them an e-mail anytime you want to. Remember, if you send them an e-mail trying to sell them... they will be gone. They can un-join your group with a click of the mouse.

There is a block option where you can block people, and they can block you. You can post to the group site where it says post a post to the group on the group page. Everybody that's in the group has access to that page. You can post things there and people that come in to view the group page will see that. The group page will have some basic information and news about the group. You can advertise your own group. You can also create a couple of groups... one for buyers - one for sellers. Then what you can do is join other groups that have similar interests and put posts in the group that say... hey, you might want to join this group too, it's about quick home fix ups for fast sale. So if you're thinking about selling you might want to hop over and join this group.

Over time, you can virally have all these people that are in other groups coming and joining your group. What you want is the ability to contact them. That is the key in this world. You want a list of people you can mail to. You can only post on the walls of groups that you join but the groups you create and are the owner of allow you to email that entire group. You have to have an audience. It doesn't matter what you're selling whether it be your real estate services or sand, if you have a big enough audience you're going to sell something.

The whole key in all this Internet stuff is you want to make your audience as big as possible, period. It doesn't matter how you get the contact info - it doesn't matter how they get in your group. You get a new listing, and you think it's time to send it out to everybody. You send it out to your three groups, which have 4300 people. You send out a broadcast e-mail to your e-mail list that you've saved on your auto responder so you can get that listing out to 10,000 people like that. And yes this does all take time to build up these lists. The social stuff, once it reaches a critical point it will mushroom by itself. You really don't have to do much else except to promote your groups to get people to join your group so that you can e-mail them. Now this is very powerful! You can also tell your Twitter people to join your group on Facebook, and they will and that gives you the ability to e-mail them too.

The Whole Picture

You search the groups… you find groups and join them. You can add friends that are in the groups if you want to. You don't have to add them as friends, but if you see people that might be in real estate in some way, form or shape you might want to friend them. They might be a carpenter or somebody relevant to your business. Recommend your group on the walls of your friends. The Wall is just a place where you can put a post just like a post message board. You can talk about your group and again if you have the benefit of the group in your group title, you can just say hey you might want to check out this group it's got some good information. Put the name of your group and the link to it. They can click on it and go right to your group. You can go to other people's groups that are similar post stuff on there and say if you like this group you might want to check out this other group because they've got good information on quick and easy fix ups. The whole idea is to generate traffic back to your group, so they can join you.

As your list grows you can email other things to your group, not just fix up tips. You can mention that you just listed this new house and to Google the address. When they do that they are going to go to one your websites with a lead capture form.

You want to set up several groups and then work to build the number of people in your groups. Your goal should be around 2500 people in your group because that gives you a big enough list to send an email to that will actually have impact because if you are only getting 1% of this that's 25 people. That's a pretty good percentage.

Usually you are going to get about 1/10 of 1% response rate on an email blast. That would be nice if you could sell a house every time you send out 2500 emails. You might have an open house coming up this weekend for your buyer group or groups depending on how many you have. You can broadcast that open house to the entire groups. You can get people to come to the open house if you set up a blog page that describes the house and has directions to it and all that stuff.

In Summary

You now understand how Twitter and Facebook can work for you. How much does it cost… it's free. Will it generate traffic for you… yes it will. It takes a little time to make it work. But let me just tell you… if you get on Twitter and just start following everybody you are going to have a bunch of noise in your Twitter box and that's it. It is just going to be noise and random posts and people frying eggs and people vacuuming… hey, I am cooking dinner now. You are going to see all kinds of junk.

That's why it's important to use that Google feature and only follow people that you think might be looking for houses or might be thinking about selling houses. That way, you've got a very targeted group of people. Facebook is the same thing. You don't want to friend everybody. You want to be a groupie. You want to join groups and tell them to join your group. Facebook you can search by city. For example, you can type in Birmingham AL on the upper right of Facebook, where the search box is. Don't just put Birmingham, because there is a Birmingham Michigan and there's a Birmingham England. Put in Birmingham AL or Birmingham Alabama. That way you're going to pull people that are in groups in Birmingham. In other words, make sure you type in your city and state or province.

Chapter 12 – Social Bookmarking

Social bookmarking is a new thing that has come out in the last couple years too. Delicious and Stumble-Upon are examples of social bookmarking sites. The list for these types of sites is growing daily and there are thousands of them by now.

Basically, it is a way for you to quickly and easily re-find things that you have already found once. However, it is also a public bookmark which means other people can look and see what you have bookmarked. If you find a great site on how to waterproof your basement that can be a big deal in your area and you want to keep it for reference. You bookmark it so that you can return to it again and again quickly and easily. You can edit tags to the items you bookmark which can be your keywords. When you add a bookmark to a site like Delicious it creates a link to the page that you were recommending. These pages can be yours or someone else's. When lots of different people bookmark a page it increases the site's popularity. The search engines notice this and the site gets ranked higher. You can't go in there and bookmark your own site 50 times it's not going to work. It will say you've already bookmarked this site, unless you have multiple accounts with different e-mail addresses. Then, you can bookmark your site 50 times and the search engines won't know any different.

Stumble-upon is the same thing as delicious. Remember there are lots of them. One of the first things you want to do is bookmark your own site. All the blogs you are going to put up - you go and bookmark them on all the different sites, the main ones are Delicious and Stumble-Upon.

There are tools out there that automate all that bookmarking. So again social bookmarking adds back links or one-way links to your site, which makes your site more popular in the search engines. Other people search for things and they can find your bookmarks. These are public bookmarks so whatever you put about your site other people can see that as well. You can also log back into your delicious account and go back and look at stuff that you bookmarked over time.

The good thing is that it does add a back link if you're doing it to your own site. The downside, you have to go and set up an account on every single social bookmarking site. Username and password, user name and password and you have to remember them all, so just make them all the same. Make it Bob for your username and Smith for your password... something easy to remember.

Note: I recommend you use the same email address for setting up social sites and create a separate email account for these as well. You don't want to use your main business email address for these.

You can also put videos up on your site and use a video tool to post them to 14 sites. You bookmark it through the social bookmarking automatic bookmarking tool. You are going to generate 80 new links to that video. This video can be hosted on your site as well.

The old way to bookmark a site was to add it to your list of favorites in your web browser. You probably have some of those where you were saving a website so you can get back to it later. The new way of bookmarking is to bookmark each site in a public place so that other people can actually see what you're bookmarking. If a site has been bookmarked a lot by numerous people it means that it must be a popular site and will be viewed as popular by Google, which is a good thing!

Something to keep in mind – When you are using all of these various tools you will end up with tons of accounts with user names and passwords to remember. One easy way is to just write them down outside your computer. I just use a notebook. You can also use tools that will remember this information for you as well.

Chapter 13 – Call Volume Explosion

What Calls Should You Answer

If you take all that you have learned and do it right, your phone will start ringing. The first rule of this business is to answer your phone! Sometimes when I am at realtor function, and I'll be standing there talking to somebody and their phone will ring and they'll look at it and say I don't know who that is and they'll ignore it. Knowing how all this information fits together, it would seem to me that that should be the call to answer. It could be someone you know and you can get back to them. On the other hand, it could be one of your leads calling because now they are ready to take action. If you are going to remember one thing in this business, then it is answer the calls where you don't know who is calling!

The second one is - see rule number one just in case you forgot.

The third rule is - if you can't answer your phone get somebody to do it or get a tool that does it for you. You have got to take the calls. Let's say you have applied everything you know thus far and your phone starts ringing. You are going to start getting phone calls from people you don't know, and you could get 30 to 50 a day. You will actually get sick and tired of answering the phone. A few years back when real estate was really hopping your phone rang off the hook. You would have to let it all go to voicemail, and then you would cherry pick through the voicemail to see which ones you wanted to work with. They sound motivated and nice I think I'll talk to them and give them some of my time. Well, it's not like that now, and you are probably wishing you had all those phones calls. The days of cherry picking the good from the grumpy ones, are not here now.

Phone Call Volume

If you're getting 30 to 50 a day, there's not enough time to answer those calls and talk to that many people. It's difficult to handle plus a lot of them are new calls that you have never had before. Here's the thing if you put your phone number on all your websites, you are going to get phone calls. They're going to come right to your cell phone, and you're going to be on one call and you got somebody else beeping in. So you can't answer them all but there is a solution.

Get a 24 hour Hotline/Assistant System

This tool is a valuable tool, but it is not free. It does cost about $25 a month, but it is amazing. Instead of putting your cell phone number on your website, this tool will answer your phone 24 hours a day seven days a week. It takes those calls and it logs in every single phone number and sends it to you by e-mail. It is a lead capture device that is awesome. All you need is the contact info and it doesn't matter if you have their name. You have their phone number, and you call them back. This thing will send and receive faxes, and it's all over the Internet. It is really cool and you should check it out.

Adtrakker

The Adtrakker system as I like to call it is a 24/7 call capture lead generation system. This system gives you a professional 1 800 number which you can start using immediately. The nice feature of this system is that it forwards your calls to any number you like. Plus it will send a notification to your e-mail for every call you receive, and it gives you their phone number. It can't get any better than that.

For every fax you receive it sends an e-mail to your primary e-mail with the fax as an attachment. Plus you can then forward that fax to somebody else if necessary. It's really good quality and it makes sending and receiving documents very easy. It cuts down on wasting paper, which is a benefit to us all. Of course you have to print something out if you need to get signatures and initials.

This system allows you to add up to five different telephone extensions for each listing. This is perfect for tracking the performance of your ad. Or you can use it to give customers more options for reaching you. If you cannot be reached, the phone system will take a voicemail for you.

Using a call tracking system allows you to put advertising messages in place. This can be a short description of the house with appropriate details. The advantage of this is that people are more likely to call to listen to a pre-recorded message as having to talk to a sales person! There is no live conversation going on but you receive an email with their phone number!

This is also a pre qualifying step. You know what type of home, the location and the price range that your new prospect was interested in. Think about it you can quickly put together a list of other properties that they might be interested in and send it to them. How's that for customer service?

With your messages you can leave a number to request a brochure or to even have you call them back. All of this can be set up automatically for each new listing that you have.

Track Your Marketing

Let's take a moment to look at a perception about marketing. I was sitting in a real estate office of a big company that used to be in business in Alabama. It was called First Real Estate, anyway you may recognize the name. I was sitting in my office one day folding newsletters. I used to send out about 4500 newsletters a month in my first year in the business here in Alabama. I did that because I've always heard that was the way to do it. Send out newsletters and let people know who you are. I bought the first digital camera and this was about 13 years ago, and people would come into my office and say man you ought to be in marketing. I would just look at them and say, "What do you think we're in." Realtors are in marketing.

Therefore, it would be good if knew a bit about marketing. Marketing is not advertising. Marketing is figuring out how to get the most bang for your buck for every dollar spent. It's how to get the most leads generated per dollar or per effort for every hour of effort that you do. That's marketing. Then measuring your conversion rates and then figuring out how many of those people that turned into prospects are going to turn into buyers or sellers. Then going all the way back and saying it cost me $192 to make a sale.

You need to learn how to measure the effectiveness of your marketing because that is what determines if you make a profit or not. If you're losing money on every deal is it worth doing? You've got to figure out a way to maximize and squeeze out the most number of prospects and the most number of closings out of every dollar you spend. That's part of business and it is something that all businesses do, realtors haven't because they don't know how.

The tracking feature of this system will make it easier and do it for you. If you are running print ads you need to know how effective these ads are. How much does each call cost you? If you have a website that you are getting phone calls from. Do you know how much do those calls cost you? You probably don't know because you don't have a way to track those calls and measure it. This system allows you this.

Here's how it works. You can put a recording for a house on extension 101… so somebody dials your 800 number and types in 101, and they'll get to hear the description of the house. Now I'm going to put that phone number and extension in the newspaper. I know how much my newspaper ad cost, and I know I can measure the exact number of phone calls I got from that newspaper ad. If you're wondering, if you're spending too much money somewhere you have to have a system like this in place so you can see how much each call cost you. If a phone call costs you a dollar, that's not too bad. If it cost you $35 that's not good, because you're not converting enough of those phone calls into actual closings.

So extension 101 will be your newspaper ad. Extension 201 is the same exact recording, and they will hear the same thing… but you will put that number and extension on your website. Extension 301 is the exact same recording, but you are putting that extension on your sign, for more detailed information right now call 1-800- ____ and press extension 301. Extension 401 could be your magazine ad. Now when you put all this out there and they all have different extension numbers, and you look at the end of the month… You can see that your newspaper ad which cost you $50 and it produced 5 calls. You can track that. You get reports and it tells you exactly how many phone calls. Your magazine ad produced 3 calls, and it cost you $499. Your website produced 6 calls, and you only pay $14 every two years for my domain name and the blog is free. Your sign writer produced 30 calls and all you had to do was pay for the sign. You can consider that sort of free too because you will have used the same sign writer at different times. Now you can accurately track exactly what's giving you your business and how much you are spending for it.

You need to know these numbers, especially in a market like this. You don't want to be wasting money on ad venues that do not produce revenue. If you're not getting enough bang for your buck stop it. If you're getting a lot of bang for your buck… do more of it. Without knowing what venue is producing the phone calls, especially if they're all going directly to your cell phone you don't know where the calls came from. You've got to have something like this system so you can track those phone calls and accurately measure what you're spending to get each one. Once you get it set up, it's very easy to look at the reports and know that you are spending $2 a call in this ad venue - spending $8 a call in this ad venue. If you're spending much more than a dollar per lead it's probably too much.

This is like having a personal assistant 24/7 to answer your calls for you and take a message and record the people's phone numbers all at one time. The cost for this tool each month is just over $20 a month, and it's worth every penny.

Chapter 14 – Other Cool Tools

oneload.com

There are other cool tools you can use to help you market, but these are not essential like the ones you have already learned. There are new free applications that are springing up all the time. This one - oneload.com it is a free service. It is hooked up to about 23 different video sharing sites. The number 1 search engine in the world right now is Google – the number 2 is YouTube, based on the number of searches done. A lot of people search for funny silly videos. oneload does require some set up. Let's say that you wanted to incorporate this as part of your marketing plan, you can produce a video on every property that you put out there. This tool can make this process easy and it is an additional way for you to showcase your information for your customers. Remember who wins in the online marketing game? The person with the most data available for their customers always wins. Video is the most you can give them without actually taking them out to the house.

You simply join oneload and follow the instructions. During the sign up process you will join several other video sharing sites. You will create new accounts at places like Viddler and Metcalfe. Just think of oneload as the central hub. I suggest you create accounts for around 10 – 14 video sharing places.

Once all your accounts are verified it is simply a matter of uploading your video once to oneload. Then oneload distributes it to all these other accounts on your behalf. Again we are setting something up once and benefitting from it.

TheFlip.com

You can make really good videos these days on a high definition video recorder. There is something called a Flip camera that works really well. You simply walk through a house and film yourself touring it. You end up making a video that is a virtual tour. You can take that video and upload it to oneload and hit submit, and it will broadcast that video to 14 video sharing sites, all at once. You are automatically going to generate 14 more links. You can go on that site and bookmark it, which provides you even more links back to your site.

The nice thing about this Flip Video Camera is that you don't have to convert it to upload it to oneload. All you do is upload it to your account and add a good title. I suggest using the address with the city and state if possible. Use specific terms so that anyone looking for a home in a particular area will find your video.

When filling in the description area always put your website address first. This will create a link from all of the video sites back to your website.

It is not just listings that you can create videos for. You could also create instructional videos for home buyers. This could be on topics of how to apply for a home loan or even step by step instructions for getting your home ready to be listed.

Socialsubmit.com

This is a social bookmarking automation tool. This is not the only social bookmarking tool that automates this whole process, there are many others as well. The downside to these social bookmarker automation programs is you do have to set an account up on every single place and save it and then copy and paste your username and password for each individual site, this can be time consuming.

But once you have it set up it becomes an automatic process. It may be well worth the effort to take the time to set up all the accounts and then use them for every listing you have.

Here's a sampling of some of the most popular bookmarking sites available today. Socialsubmit acts as the central location. Can you imagine having to log into each account separately, it would take days!

Automatic social bookmarking

Backflip	BlinkBits	Blinklist	blogmarks	Buddymarks	CiteUlike
del.icio.us	de.lirio.us	digg	Tip'd	Feed Me Links!	Furl
Gibeo	Gravee	Hyperlinkomatic	igooi	kinja	Lilisto
Linkagogo	Linkroll	looklater	Magnolia	maple	MesFavs
netvouz	Newsvine	Raw Sugar	reddit	Rojo	Scuttle
Segnalo	Shadows	Simpy	Spurl	Squidoo	tagtooga
Tailrank	Technorati	unalog	Wink	wists	Yahoo M Web
zurpy	FeedMarker	Health Ranker			

What is SocialSubmit?

SocialSubmit allows you to easily submit a link to several social bookmarking si

Recap - What you're trying to do is to set up different tracking funnels to end up at the same place. You're going to use social bookmarking and hopefully get some traffic to your Facebook page, which is going to in turn hopefully send traffic to your real website, your real estate website. That is a traffic funnel right there. Twitter, can be another traffic funnel that you can send traffic to your web/blog page. Without traffic your site's dead, it is as though you don't exist.

You have to have ways to get people to come look at your web/blog page, so they can find your contact information and fill in your lead capture form. That's the whole key here.

With Facebook you want to have a separate page for your listings so that you can bookmark it to create more links. The same idea goes with videos you want to bookmark each video to all the various bookmarking sites. Your videos contain your website address so people know where to go for more information.

In essence what you are doing is generating traffic from as many different sources as possible. This will capture leads for you and when this happens you follow up with your automatic systems in place.

Landing Page

The last thing you are going to learn is all about a landing page. You should have some of your free blogs set up as landing pages or another term for that is a squeeze page. This is nothing more than one page that has one purpose and that is getting the people to put their information into your form. That's it. You can set this up on the blogging platform at blogger. You can do it on WordPress but remember a landing page is like a blog with one post, that's it. The one post is an advertisement for something that you can allow people to get for free by putting in their name and their e-mail and clicking that submit button. Then they go into your automatic follow-up sequence. They get whatever it is they want for free, and then you're going to follow up with them automatically. It's a lead generation page and that's all it is.

You are going to want to use the AIDA - attention, interest, desire and action - formula to follow setting up your landing page. You have to have something of value you are going to offer them… that ethical bribe.

It can be unlimited access to homes in your area that are listed or get instant unrestricted access to the homes listed in your area. That's the number one thing that people want. Out of everybody searching for houses on the Internet the number one thing that they want, is access to your database, that's it. On your landing page, you tell them the benefits and features of instant MLS access. Once they click submit if you have changed the success URL to your regular website that already has MLS search on it, and they click that submit button it will take them right to your site, so they can search MLS. Your landing page is the page to capture the lead once it's captured you got to give them what they came for.

What you can do is you can set up a blog where you talk about that. "If you want unlimited, unrestricted access 24/7 anytime you want to get all you have to do is put in your name and e-mail address, and you will instantly be taken to a page where you can get on and search the whole area MLS."

To do this you follow the same process that we did when we were looking at the code for the auto responder that you copy and pasted into your JavaScript HTML box? Remember the success URL, and put your own website in there because you want to keep your visitor on the same page?

If you want them to go to a MLS search portal that's the address you would put in there. You direct them to your landing page. That's where you want to send traffic to so you can capture their name and e-mail and when they click submit it will automatically take them to your website that already has MLS search on it. That's that success URL that we talked about it, and it's in the form for the free autobot auto responder. When you copy and paste that code it's going to be in red, and you have to replace it with something so that will remind you to put that in there.

Most people already have a website set up that allows people to go straight to it and search MLS. If you already have a website, you're not keeping people out of MLS because they can go on there and search anytime they want. That feature is already set up. The problem is they've got their traffic going straight to their website. You want to go to a landing page so you can squeeze that information out of them and then let them get to your main website. That's the whole key here you want to capture the lead. You give me something, I'll give you something. If you send them straight to your website, you are not getting their contact information so you can later follow up with them.

You don't have to use MLS access as your bribe. You can use any kind of ethical bribe that has value for these people. Any kind of added value you can think of. Look on the Internet and remember you can go to that NAR website to find reports. Find information that people would like to get, and you can set up landing pages for each info piece that you can find. Then put the form for your auto responder and have the auto responder instantly e-mail them for whatever, they've asked for.

Once again, these pages are free, and you can have as many as you want. There is no charge. It's all free, especially if you're using the free auto responder. I would recommend you get a paid one if you're going to do a lot of this because you can include attachments and videos. Make sure to ask for their name and e-mail. After they click on the submit button send your bribe immediately so they get what they requested without having to wait.

Here's an example of a landing page.

Preferred Access makes a big difference...
                              Get Access now!

The Real Estate Catch 22

How to Trade Up without Moving Twice

Every month, thousands of homeowners are faced with the stressful dilemma of whether to buy f owning two homes. Or, just as bad, if you sell first, you could end up homeless. It's what insiders position to find yourself in.

This financial and emotional tightrope is one you usually have to walk alone because most agents created a unique **Guaranteed Sale Program** which solves this dilemma. This program guarantee your home doesn't sell in 120 days, they will buy it from you themselves for the previously agreed

Before you hire any professional, you should research the market to find out who can do the bes are willing to give you with respect to the selling of your home. **In a market where many home which ensures that your home will sell is critical**. Unfortunately, you'll find that most agents :

To help you learn more about this program and how it can make your move less stressful, a FREE *Twice*".

Order this report NOW to find out how to guarantee the cash sale of your home.

     Your Contact Information (Please complete all fields)
       First Name: EMail:

You might have seen this one before. It is actually a page from a website put out by Craig Proctor's group. This is one of their famous lead capture pages. You can go to a lot of websites and click on how to avoid the six biggest mistakes homebuyers make. It will be on the left menu bar, and it will take you to this landing page. Obviously, it gives you the benefit, gets your attention, builds your interest, makes you want it, and then it tells you how to get it. Attention, interest, desire and action.

Once you fill in your name and e-mail address you click submit and the report is e-mailed to you. Of course you are also hooked up now to an auto responder, and you're going to get e-mail forever from this agent. It has one purpose and only one purpose. It's not ambiguous at all. It's pretty clear what we want. If you want this fill this out. That's the whole key to this is, make a compelling offer and then say… and guess what it's free. All they have to do is fill out this form and click submit, and you'll have it within seconds.

Here's another one. The Six mistakes to avoid when moving to a larger home.

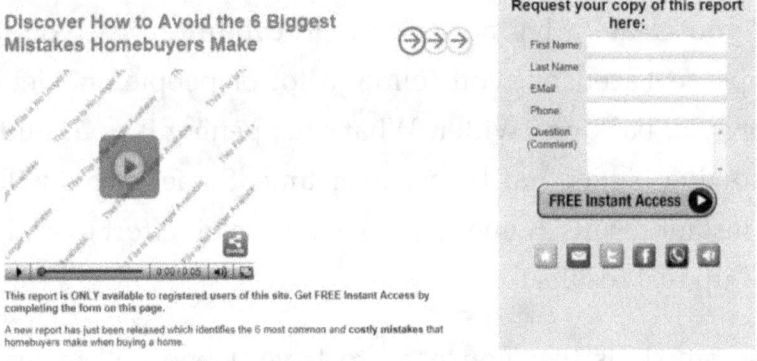

This one has to do with having to move twice when you trade up. A lot of people are wondering, which came first the chicken or the egg. What do you do when… you have to move out of your house and sell it or sell it and move out, and then you can start looking for another one? This report addresses that. This is popular among people who want to move up in price range. Again, there is no ambiguity here. Your offer addresses that they are looking for – simple.

Another thing you can do on your landing page with that Flip camera is, make a video of yourself talking about your offer. You can put that video up, and you can say… all you have to do to get this free report is, fill out the form that's right under my video." You can upload it directly to your blog and people will fill out your form as long as they get what you've offered in your lead capture or your landing page.

Remember… you can sell anything if your audience is big enough. So you're going to have to create a big audience. The way you create a big audience is to capture leads, you create groups on Facebook, you follow a lot of people and let them follow you back on Twitter. What's happening is your audience is growing bigger and bigger over time. Some of this will give you instant results. Some of it takes a little bit effort over time to build up real results from.

These are skills that you need to have. I know it's a learning curve. It was a learning curve when you got in the business. Nothing stays the same. This business always changes and nothing stays the same. Our customers' behavior has changed, we have to adapt to it.

Summary

In summary, you want to set up some kind of system for follow-up, and you want to automate as many of the pieces of the follow-up puzzle as you can. I'm going to suggest again the best way to do it is to set up action plans and set up about seven categories of people. That is the best way to do it... I have never seen a better way. Those action plans make it easy because you don't have to worry what comes next.

Then you want to automate the e-mail part of it - you want to automate broadcasts from your group - and you want to automate Twitter tweets.

If you're going to gather information when you talk to these people one-on-one, you want to just concentrate on family, organization, recreation and dreams. Because then these people will think that you're actually interested in them not just their money. If you ask about what price range, that's money. If you say how much money do you have? That's money. If you say how many children do you have, that doesn't have anything to do with money, and they will start talking to you and you'll find out all you need to know about these people. So concentrate on family, organization, recreation and dreams. You're going to get information that will bind these customers to you because nobody else is going to ask for that kind of stuff.

Once your actions start to kick in you want to look at something like Adtrakker, so you have a system to field your calls. My phone quit ringing a long time ago, has anybody else had that problem? Customers suddenly went quiet. If people find you on the Internet, they will start calling you as long as you've got a reason for them to call.

You want to use social media to generate more leads. I'm talking about Twitter and Facebook. There are many other social media applications, which we didn't cover here. There's just too many of them, and they're cropping up all over the place. Those are two most popular, and they've actually got applications that can help you manage them. Like that tweet later thing and the Google search feature for Twitter. That allows you to target people that you want to follow.

You want to drive traffic to your lead capture or landing pages so that you generate leads, and they go into your e-mail auto responder so you can follow up with these people.

Make your e-mails personal. If you don't know how to write personal messages talk to your prospects as though you were talking to a good friend or writing your spouse an email. You want your emails to be remembered the way a great conversation is remembered. The tone of your e-mails should be chatty and personal. Believe me, it will make a huge difference in your business.

Writing in this way is a difficult skill to acquire, but if you get good at that and you can write just like you talk, you are going to get a lot higher response rate from your e-mails because people are going to feel like you're actually talking to them.

Just remember - you want to market smarter... not sell harder. That is the key to your whole business success.

To Your Success
Mike Carraway